Scouts

The stories that built a movement

To every Scout, past, present and future.

A STUDIO PRESS BOOK

First published in the UK in 2019 by Studio Press,
an imprint of Bonnier Books UK,
The Plaza, 535 King's Road, London SW10 0SZ

www.studiopressbooks.co.uk
www.bonnierbooks.co.uk

1 3 5 7 9 10 8 6 4 2

ISBN 978-1-78741-554-6

Edited by Sophie Blackman
Designed by Steve Leard (Leard.co.uk) and Rob Ward

A CIP catalogue for this book is available from the British Library
Printed and bound in Turkey

With a foreword by Bear Grylls

Scouts

The stories that built a movement

Contents

Foreword

I'm so proud to introduce the story of the Scouts, one of the greatest youth movements the world has ever known.

The Scouts began with a single, brilliant idea – to bring young people together from different backgrounds and help them develop skills for life. Over 110 years later we're still doing that, but on an almost unimaginable scale. Today I'm so proud that 50 million Scouts are developing new skills, making new friends and setting out on new adventures. These Scouts are the leaders of the future – resilient, determined and filled with hope for a better world. Whenever I meet Scouts on my travels, I'm always so inspired by their courage, optimism and endeavour.

Back in 1907, our founder, Robert Baden-Powell, tested his idea for the Scouts with the experimental camp on Brownsea Island in Poole Harbour, UK. He brought together young people from different walks of life, encouraging them to understand and learn from each other. He shared stories from his travels across the world and helped them discover the names for the constellations, animals and plants. He knew early on that the outdoors was the world's greatest classroom. Working in Patrols, they worked and played together, always supporting each other. He wrote up the results in his book, *Scouting for Boys*, which went on to sell millions of copies worldwide.

Today, we are proud to welcome both boys and girls into the movement, from all backgrounds. In other words: Scouting is for all. We are united by a spirit of peace and unity that transcends borders and which we carry throughout our lives. We are united too by our promise to do our best and help other people. From supporting our communities in times of crisis to welcoming refugees, above all, it is kindness that marks out a Scout from the crowd. We don't just put up tents, we build character.

You will read some incredible stories in this book: how the Scouts rose to the challenge during the world wars, taking in the harvest and acting as coastguards; you will see how the movement went underground in war-torn countries, and gave hope to the oppressed and imprisoned. You will also witness its rapid expansion to every corner of the globe.

As we look ahead to the challenges of the future, it's Scouts who remain our shining lights, still leading the way.

**Bear Grylls
UK Chief Scout and Chief Ambassador of World Scouting**

It's hard to image a world without Scouts, but of course it had to start somewhere. In 1907, Robert Baden-Powell tried out his simple but revolutionary idea. It was about getting young people together in small teams, helping them to learn skills together and to experience the magic of the outdoors. It proved a winning formula. Young people loved their newfound freedom, sense of independence and responsibility, and flocked to the new movement.

Part 1

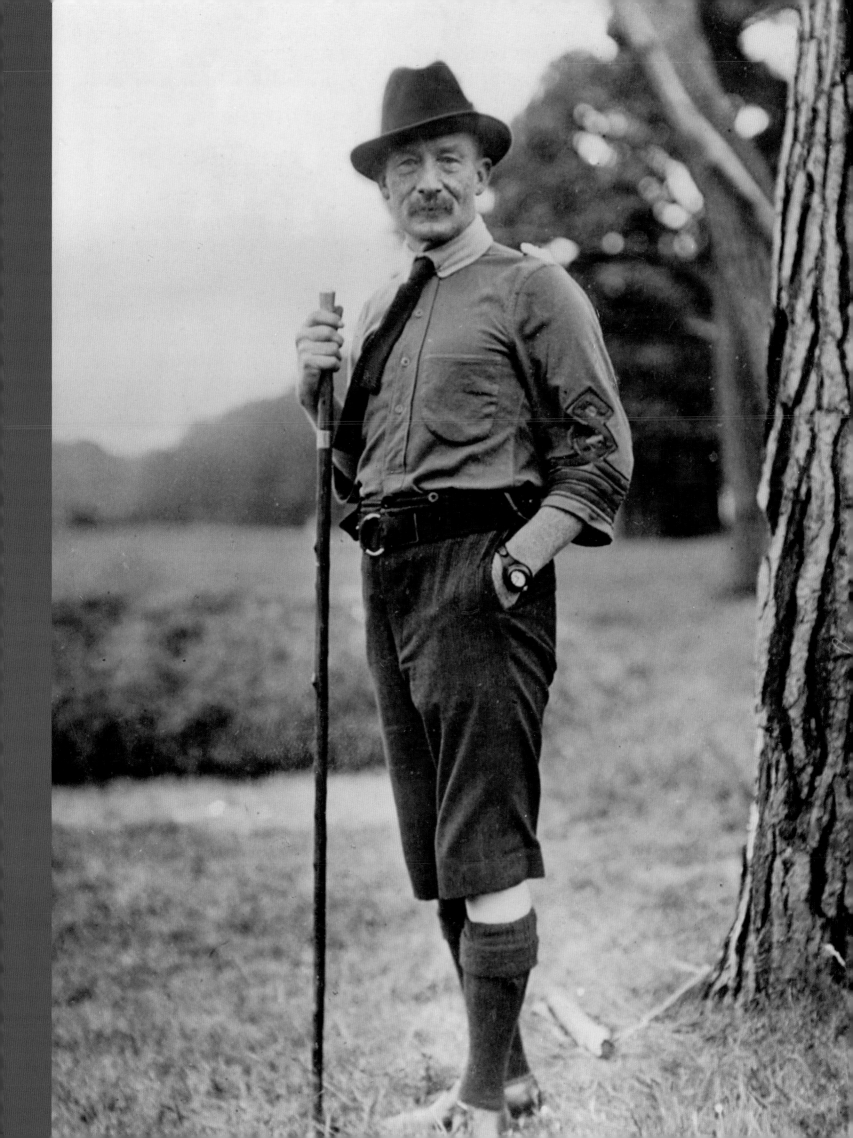

The early years

Baden-Powell, top centre, with his brothers and sisters.

Baden-Powell's childhood

The period between 1850 and 1950 saw the greatest social change in England in any century. This also coincided with Baden-Powell's lifetime.

Victorian England

In the 1850s and into the 20th century, men wore hats in public – silk top hats, bowlers or boaters – and gentlemen carried canes (walking sticks). Their dress was formal and their collars were stiff. Horse-drawn carriages, cabs and omnibuses would gradually be replaced with bicycles and new motorcars in the following decades. This was still a world where lamplighters lit up the street lights each night by hand, and straw was strewn in front of a house where someone was ill to deaden traffic noise. Most houses were lit by gas or oil lamps.

Although there was peace and prosperity at this time in Britain, there was also great poverty. In the East End of London, one-third of the population lived in poverty. Drunkenness was rife, and hungry, dirty, barefoot children were commonplace. Thousands of Londoners, many under sixteen years old, lived on the streets.

At the other end of the social scale, the very wealthy lived in comparative ease and luxury. In between, there were the middle classes. These respectable citizens were driven by their work ethic and social conscience, with a dire warning of poverty on one side, and the possibility of great wealth on the other. Many of the middle classes aimed to better themselves, either by marriage or hard work.

At the turn of the century, most children left school at the age of 12, but many were out working long before that. They also played games in the street and collected pictures of their heroes. It was a country of sharp social division, and Scouting, the vision of Robert Baden-Powell, was designed to bridge the gap.

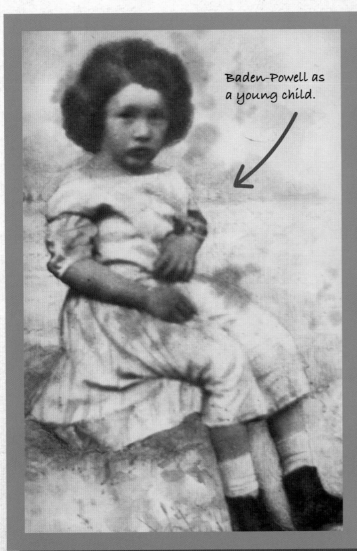

Baden-Powell as a young child.

A child of his time

Robert Stephenson Smyth Powell, the future Scout Founder, was born on 22 February 1857, at 6 Stanhope Street (now 11 Stanhope Terrace), near Paddington station in London. He was christened a few days later in St James's Church nearby. His father, the Reverend Baden Powell, was an Oxford clergyman and academic. He was the first cleric to declare openly his support for Darwinian evolutionary theory. Author of *The Order of Nature*, Powell did considerable harm to his own career by holding such scientific views about creation.

Professor Powell had been married and widowed twice before. He had four children by his first wife when he married Henrietta Grace Smyth. She was one of the six daughters and three sons of Captain William Henry Smyth, a naval captain (later Admiral) and a senior member of the Royal Astronomical Society. It was through science that Professor Powell met Captain Smyth and his daughter in Oxford. Powell and Henrietta Grace married in 1846, when she was 21 and he was 48.

They had ten children together before Professor Powell died in 1860. Four of the children died in childhood, as was sadly common in those days, even in wealthier families. The death of his favourite older brother, Augustus, left young Robert bereft.

Changing the name

As a tribute to her late husband, but principally as a means of social advancement, Henrietta had her husband's first name, Baden, added to the family surname to create the new double-barrelled surname of Baden-Powell. This produced slightly ludicrous results for her stepson, Baden Henry Powell, who didn't use the new surname, and her youngest son, Baden, who became Baden Baden-Powell. 'Remember to help others,' she told them. 'We cannot be good ourselves unless we are always helping others.' Her son, Robert, would remember this message later in his life when he introduced the 'daily good turn' to Scouting.

Baden-Powell at school

As a young boy, Robert was educated at home, and he then attended a preparatory school in Kensington. At the age of 11, he then went to his father's old school, Rose Hill, near Tunbridge Wells in Kent. His reports noted his progress, saying that his conduct was 'very good'. From here, having turned down a place at Fettes College, Edinburgh, he won a scholarship to one of Britain's leading public schools. At the time, Charterhouse School was based near St Paul's Cathedral in London, but after two years there, Robert moved with his school to new premises in Godalming, Surrey. This new environment allowed him to develop his love of the outdoors and his skills in tracking.

But young Baden-Powell did not do so well in his studies: Baden-Powell 'has to all intents given up the study of mathematics' wrote one teacher in his report; 'often sleeps in class' wrote another!

However, Baden-Powell excelled at sport, and at football in particular. He also joined the school's newly formed Band and Rifle Corps, and played the piano, fiddle, bugle and the flugelhorn, sang in the choir and was a member of the school's shooting team. Inheriting his mother's artistic talent, he excelled as an artist, producing sketches and watercolours. His other great talent was for acting; he performed in more than 20 school productions. He wrote frequently for the school magazine, joined the debating and literary society and became a member of a secret club of 12 senior students called the Druids, where he was nicknamed 'Lord Bathing Towel'!

During the school holidays, he and his brothers enjoyed themselves fishing, racing, wildfowling and sailing. The naval base at Portsmouth was a favourite haunt of theirs, but they also sailed further to the harbours of Southampton, Bournemouth and Poole, passing by Brownsea Island, and inland to trace the source of the River Thames.

B-P sketched his fellow classmates sitting their exams.

'Laws for me when I am old'

Robert was known as Stephe, pronounced 'Stevie', within his family. And at the age of eight, Stephe wrote a statement of his beliefs for his grandfather, which he titled 'Laws for me when I am old'. It was the early basis for a code of values that he would live by for the rest of his life, and which would find later echoes in the Scout Law and Promise.

> I will have the poor people to be as rich as we are, and they ought by rights to be as happy as we are, and all who go across the crossings shall give the poor crossing sweeper some money and you ought to thank God for what he has given us and he made the poor people to be poor and the rich people to be rich and I can tell you how to be good. Now I will tell you. You must pray to God whenever you can but you cannot be good with only praying but you must try very hard to be good.
> By R.S.S. Powell, Feb 26th 1865.'

Next steps

Any thought of becoming a professional actor or artist was squashed by his mother, and in 1876, Baden-Powell went to Oxford to sit the university entrance exams, hoping to follow in the footsteps of his father and brothers. He was rejected by both Balliol and Christ Church Colleges but signed up as a non-attached student.

Then he came across the announcement for an Open Competitive Examination for commissions in the army, into both infantry and cavalry regiments. He had not previously given much thought to an army career, and there was no precedent in his immediate family history.

When he was only just enough, Baden-Powell sat the preliminary exams in London – arithmetic and geometry, French, geography and written English. He progressed to the next stage, choosing four subjects from a choice of mathematics, English composition, Latin, Greek, French, German, science, geography and free-hand drawing. When the results were published, out of 718 candidates, Baden-Powell was placed fifth for the infantry and second for cavalry, gaining 5,350 marks out of a possible 11,300.

Flying colours

On 11 September 1876, Baden-Powell received his Army commission. Successful candidates were usually sent for two years of further study at the Royal Military College at Sandhurst. However, in this instance, the first six candidates were excused and immediately assigned to regiments to be posted overseas. Baden-Powell joined the crack 13th Hussars and was ordered to North India, where the regiment was stationed. He sailed from England on 30 October 1876. The next day, Queen Victoria would be proclaimed Empress of India.

Baden-Powell's influences

Baden-Powell was always interested in people, and he enjoyed listening to their stories and ideas. The following people had an influence on him and his thinking and played a part in the development of Scouting.

Father: Professor Baden Powell
(1796–1860)

The Reverend Professor Baden Powell died in June 1860, when his son Robert was only three years old. A courageous cleric with a scientific mind, he believed that fossil remains proved that Bible stories of creation could not be taken literally. Professor Powell published *The Order of Nature*, a book admired by Charles Darwin. B-P agreed with the arguments for evolution, and that 'improvement' was dependent on fitness and adaptation to surroundings. B-P's focus on physical well-being and alert intelligence matched well with the 'social Darwinism' that became popular after his father's book was published.

Step-brother: Baden Henry Powell
(1841–1901)

Baden Henry Powell, the eldest son of Professor Powell, was a legal scholar. He became a judge in the Indian High Court and an authority on land ownership. Baden was a natural draughtsman and enthusiastic amateur artist, and he submitted paintings to the Simla Academy Exhibition. B-P later did the same, following in his footsteps. Baden Henry Powell wrote the book *The Manufactures and Arts of the Punjab*, and was connected with the Kipling family through this fascination with 'arts and crafts'. Rudyard Kipling's father, Lockwood, was curator of the Central Musuem in Lahore, and Powell was an enthusiastic supporter of the museum. They were seven years apart in age, and had only their late father and a love of drawing in common, but B-P later depended on Baden to support him socially and financially when he went out to India in 1876 to join the 13th Hussars.

Commanding Officer: Lord Roberts
(1832–1914)
Frederick Sleigh Roberts, Field Marshal Lord Roberts of Kandahar, was known simply as 'Bobs'. He was the commanding officer when B-P served in India in 1880. Roberts had won great acclaim for his leadership in Kandahar, Afghanistan. 'Bobs of Kandahar' was B-P's Commander-in-Chief again in South Africa, and he made B-P responsible for the South African Constabulary following his successful defence of Mafeking in 1899. Roberts was supportive of the Scouts. He was a founding father of the National Service League and helped create Britain's first official secret service. B-P sent Roberts the earliest draft of *Scouting for Boys* for his comments. Roberts then introduced B-P to Ernest Thompson Seton to discuss starting up groups of Woodcraft Indians in the UK. Roberts, Kipling and Baden-Powell formed a triangle of friendship and had a great effect on each other's lives.

Friend: Ernest Thompson Seton
(1860–1946)

Ernest Seton's ideas on the natural world contributed to Scouting. He grew up in Toronto and, fascinated by the lifestyle of Native Americans, would escape to the wilderness to build camps and observe wildlife. He later became a naturalist, a wildlife illustrator and an anatomist.

In 1902, the *Ladies Home Journal* asked Seton to write about his organisation, the Woodcraft Indians, and Kipling encouraged him to write fiction. B-P had been working on a handbook, but reading Seton's *The Birch-bark Roll of the Woodcraft Indians* (1906) sharpened his focus. He adapted some of Seton's ideas, including totem poles and non-competitive skills badges, and drew from other sources too. Seton wanted to bring his organisation to the UK, so Lord Roberts introduced him to B-P, and they met in London in 1906. Seton later became the first Chief Scout of the Boy Scouts of America.

Friend: Rudyard Kipling
(1865–1936)

B-P and Kipling probably met for the first time in Lahore in 1883 when B-P was visiting his step-brother. They met again in South Africa as Kipling was writing the *Just So Stories*. These included 'The Tabu Tale' about a girl whose father teaches her to scout. B-P discussed with Kipling his idea for turning *Aids to Scouting for NCOs and Men* into a book for 'civilian use'. Kipling supported B-P's movement and allowed B-P to quote from his books. *Kim* (1899) was quoted many times in *Scouting for Boys*. Kipling also wrote the 'Boy Scouts' Patrol Song' for the 1909 Crystal Palace Rally.

B-P later used Kipling's *Jungle Books* for *The Wolf Cubs Handbook*. When B-P was made a Baron, Kipling said he had 'changed the outlook of Young England in the last 12 years'. Kipling was later made honorary Commissioner of Cub Scouts. In response, he created the *Land and Sea Tales for Scouts and Guides* (1923).

Brownsea Island

On 29 July 1907, 20 boys arrived on Brownsea Island for what was to be the first experimental Scout camp. The next eight days would become the most momentous camp ever held.

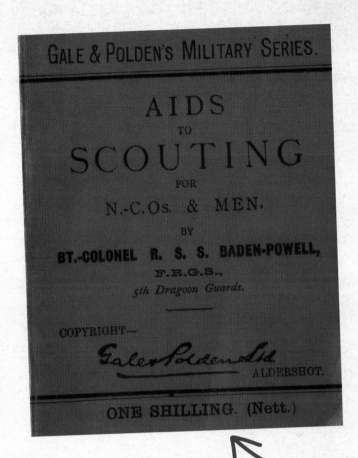

Programme of activities

Baden-Powell returned from the Boer War a national hero. As well as being a soldier, he was also an author, and he had published a military manual called *Aids to Scouting*, which contained training exercises for military scouts. This book became popular with younger boys who mimicked the exercises.

B-P had seen first-hand that a lot of young men joined the army with a lack of knowledge about nutrition and fitness. There was also an appetite in England at the time for a scheme that trained young people, so that they could play active roles in their communities from an early age.

With this in mind, B-P drafted a version of his book for boys, which swapped the military focus for one on adventure, exploration and survival. He then tested these ideas by running an experimental camp for boys. He didn't set out to start a new movement, but simply to provide a programme of activities for use by existing youth organisations, such as the Boys' Brigade.

The experimental camp

Baden-Powell chose the 20 boys aged ten to 16 years old from a cross-section of society, which was revolutionary at the time, as Britain was more divided by class than it is today. He ensured that all activities could be enjoyed by the most privileged to the poorest.

The camp was located on Brownsea Island in Poole Harbour on the south coast of England, where B-P had sailed as a boy. After a chance encounter in May 1907 with the island's owner, Charles van Raalte, B-P secured the site for his camp.

When the boys arrived on the island, tents had been pitched and a flag stood in the middle of the camp. The boys were divided into four Scout Patrols: Wolves, Bulls, Curlews and Ravens. The nearest thing to a uniform was a coloured 'shoulder knot' that indicated which Patrol each boy belonged to: yellow for Curlews, red for Ravens, blue for Wolves and green for Bulls.

The Patrol Leaders each wore a short staff with a white flag bearing a picture of their Patrol animal, which Baden-Powell himself had painted. They also wore a fleur-de-lis badge on the front of their hats. B-P had used this symbol with his army scouts, and a modified version would later become known as the Scout Badge.

The programme

The eight-day programme began on 1 August 1907 and was designed to teach the boys key skills and noble values, such as chivalry and discipline.

The first day began with Baden-Powell rousing the camp by blowing on the kudu horn, a souvenir of his expedition to the Somabula Forest during the 1896 Matabele Campaign. After a quick wash, some cocoa, a short demonstration and a brief session of physical drill, the flag was hoisted, prayers were said and breakfast was eaten. Then the boys started on their programme of Scouting exercises.

Most of the techniques had been taken from B-P's army training during the Boer War. He taught the Scouts by allowing them to experiment first: 'Make each boy lay a fire in his own way and light it. After failures, show them the right way (i.e. delicate use of dry chips and shavings, and sticks in a pyramid) and make them do it again.'

Brownsea Island Camp

Day 1 – Preliminary
Settling into camp
Formation of Patrols
Distribution of duties, orders, etc.
Each subject of the course explained with demonstrations
Patrol Leaders received a special course of instruction in the field to impart subsequently to their Patrols

Day 2 – Campaigning
Camp resourcefulness
Hut and hat making
Knots, fire lighting, cooking, health and sanitation, endurance
Finding way in strange country
Boat management

Day 3 – Observation
Noticing and memorising details far and near landmarks, etc.
Tracking
Deducing meaning from tracks and signs
Training eyesight, etc.

Day 4 – Woodcraft
Study of animals and birds, plants, stars, etc.
Stalking animals
Noticing details of people, reading their character and condition, thereby gaining sympathy

Day 5 – Chivalry
Honour
Code of the Knights
Unselfishness
Courage
Charity and thrift
Loyal to King and to Employers or Officers
Practical chivalry to women
Obligation to do a 'good turn' daily, and how to do it, etc.

Day 6 – Saving Life
From fire, drowning, sewer gas, runaway horses, panic, street accidents, etc.
Improvised apparatus, First Aid, Albert Medal, etc.

Day 7 – Patriotism
Colonial geography, history and deeds that won the empire
Our navy and army
Flags
Medals
Duties as citizen
Marksmanship
Helping Police, etc.

Day 8 – Games
Sports comprising games or competitive practices in all subjects of the course

A movement is born

On 9 August, the boys returned home exhausted and exhilarated. The great adventure had come to an end. The groups of boys had lived, worked and played together in a way that would not have been thought possible on the mainland due to their differences in class. The success of the camp had exceeded Baden-Powell's expectations in every way and he was ready to take his idea to a wider audience.

Baden-Powell and the boys prepare for a game.

Kit list

Each boy was requested to bring a camp kit, rolled up in a waterproof sheet or valise with straps.

Knife, fork and spoon
2 enamelled plates & 1 mug
Waterproof sheet
2 blankets (no sheets)
1 pillow and p. case
2 rough towels
1 smooth Towel
Tin cooking 'Billy' *
Canvas haversack *
Jack knife and lanyard *
2 coat straps 8" long *
Soap & sponge
Toothbrush
Brush & comb
Small looking glass

* Optional. Can be bought in camp at low price if desired.

The boys also had to bring clothing packed in a handbag or canvas 'dirty clothes' bag.

1 pair flannel trousers
1 pair flannel 'shorts' or knickerbockers
2 pairs stockings & garters (if possible with green tabs showing below the roll of stockings)
2 Flannel shirts
Neckerchief (preferably dark green)
1 suit pyjamas
1 pair bathing drawers
Sweater or old jacket
Cap
Hat; preferably grey wideawake, for sun
2 pairs strong boots or shoes
1 pair slippers or canvas shoes

The Scout emblem

As Scouting spread around the world, so too did the emblem. Some prefer the name 'arrowhead', avoiding the fleur-de-lis's royal connections, while others prefer the name 'fleur-de-lis', avoiding the military connotations of 'arrowhead'. Regardless of its name, this symbol unites Scouts worldwide.

On Brownsea Island in August 1907, Baden-Powell gave the boys a Scout symbol to wear on their coats or hats. This was based on a badge he had introduced to the Army scouts when he was serving in India.

1907

'The Scout emblem is the arrow head, which shows the north on a map or on the compass. It is the badge of the scout in the Army because he shows the way: so, too, a peace Scout shows the way in doing his duty and helping others.' Baden-Powell, Scouting for Boys (1908)

1908

Illustration from Scouting for Boys, 1908. Following criticisms that the symbol was too militaristic, Baden-Powell renamed the symbol after the fleur-de-lis, a lily that symbolised peace and purity.

In 1909, two stars were added to the otherwise generic design to make it unique to Scouting.

1909

The ten points of the stars came to represent the ten parts of the Scout Law. In the UK there were only nine Scout laws until 1911.

After the formal creation of the Wolf Cubs in 1916, the two stars also represented the gleaming eyes of a wolf cub. During the programme, Wolf Cubs worked to earn two stars for their caps. Wolf Cubs are born blind – and new Cubs have no stars on their caps. But by the time a Cub is ready to go to Scouts, he will have earnt two stars and his eyes have opened fully.

1911

1916

The symbol kept evolving with subtle changes to the shape, and in 1927, the words 'Boy Scouts' were added.

1927

In 1972, the World Membership Badge was introduced for all national Scout organisations that belonged to the World Organization of the Scout Movement (WOSM).

1972

This UK Scout logo was introduced in 2001, and with minor colour changes remained in place until May 2018.

2001

In 2018, a new brand identity was introduced for UK Scouts. This included a simplified fleur-de-lis, visible on phones and other devices. It was an evolution of the classic symbol for the digital age. This new fleur-de-lis is now seen on signs, books, clothing, social media and websites.

2018

Scouting for Boys

Even before Baden-Powell ran his experimental camp on Brownsea Island, he had started work on the manuscript that would become his most famous book: Scouting for Boys.

After the camp, B-P took what he had learnt and spend the next few months on his next book. He began by sketching out some of his initial thoughts in two pamphlets: *Boy Scouts: a Suggestion* and *Boy Scouts: Summary of Scheme*, which he had published and circulated to a few friends. In these, he summarised the essential Scout skills, the training required and the organisation of the Scouts into Patrols, and Patrols into a Troop under a Scoutmaster. But, he noted, expenses would be very small, 'no apparatus or uniform is absolutely necessary beyond badges' and that an 'inexpensive handbook called *Scouting for Boys* is being prepared'.

Baden-Powell was free to concentrate on writing from 1907, as his time as Inspector-General of Cavalry finished after he had completed a tour of Egypt and the Sudan. The first third of his original manuscript survives as handwritten scraps of paper. In June 1907 he spent time writing at the Izaak Walton Hotel in Dovedale, Derbyshire, and met with Arthur Pearson, his publisher, to discuss the best way of spreading his ideas to the wider public.

Together they worked out a programme for the next 12 months. If Baden-Powell's experimental camp was a success, he would tour the UK during the winter of 1907 to 1908 explaining his scheme. In the meantime, Pearson would publish *Scouting for Boys*. Pearson also provided £1,000 to cover initial expenses and provided office space in Henrietta Street, London. They also planned to produce *The Scout* magazine in 1908.

Cottage by the windmill

Baden-Powell returned to writing, borrowing a cottage situated next to a windmill on Wimbledon Common, where he stayed for ten days. By writing both in his own hand and dictating to a succession of shorthand writers, he completed his first draft. The cottage was owned at the time by a Mrs Fetherstonhaugh, whom he had met while with his uncle in Malta. It had its own menagerie of penguins, owls and lemurs!

Spreading the word

Much of Baden-Powell's time during November and December was taken up with the lecture tour that had been agreed with Pearson. At the first meeting, held in Hereford on 8 November 1907, he told his audience that this was the beginning of his 'crusade' with a two-fold purpose.

First, to convince the public of the urgent need for some kind of character training for young people, and second, to expound the idea of Scouting as a means of attracting boys to existing organisations, or to a new body: the Boy Scouts. He was an excellent speaker with good humour and wit, and many stories of real adventures. At first, he used hand-drawn diagrams to illustrate his points, but when the scheme was more developed, a Boy Scout on the platform helped him explain the details of the uniform and badges.

In these two months, Baden-Powell lectured in Swansea, Radcliffe, Exeter, Carlisle, Glasgow, Edinburgh, Scarborough and London. By February 1908 he had delivered 50 such lectures to great acclaim.

First publication

Scouting for Boys was published in six parts, each costing 4d (about 2p) per copy. The first part appeared on 15 January 1908, the others at fortnightly intervals. Its cover picture showed a Scout with hat and stave, lying low behind a rock, observing a smugglers' ship in the distance – which promised young readers not just tales of adventure but the chance to experience them too.

The text was a ragbag of short chapters and articles from a wide range of sources, illustrated with sketches by the author. There were games to be played and stories to be read, and there were details of the Scout Promise, the Scout Law and of the Scout uniform. This sort of patchwork-style book appealed to boys with even the shortest attention span.

Interspersing 'yarns' drawing from the works of Rudyard Kipling, Sir Arthur Conan-Doyle and Native American culture, with practical advice and woodcraft, Scouting for Boys was the original 'adventure handbook'. Scouts could find out how to stop a runaway horse, track and catch a thief, make a straw mattress and 'drag an insensible man'.

With 'tips for instructors' as well as addressing young people themselves, B-P succeeded in creating a 'one size fits all' manual – pulling off that rare trick of appealing to several audiences at the same time.

He had an uncanny knack for knowing what young boys wanted: plenty of practical skills as well as blood and gore, perhaps accounting for the stories of a man tumbling to his death over Niagara Falls, a double fatality on a railway line and the hanging of a murderer. It was his tone, above all, that endeared him to his young readership: funny, companionable and never patronising.

A runaway bestseller

The fortnightly editions sold so well that shortly after the final part had been published, a complete edition containing a slightly revised text appeared in May 1908, in both a cloth-covered hardback and as a paperback. It reprinted a further five times that year. Its sales were phenomenal and as Scouting spread, the book was translated into many languages – French, Italian, German, Chinese, Japanese and Hebrew to name but a few. It continues in print to this day, making it one of the world's bestselling books.

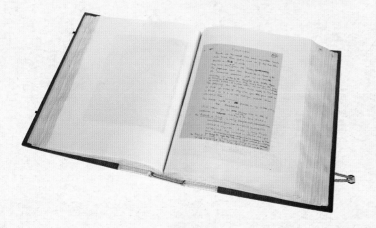

Scouting is born

By the end of January 1908, the response to the book and lectures was so great Baden-Powell became convinced of the need for an organisation dedicated to delivering the activity programme. An announcement was made at a YMCA HQ in Birkenhead, and the movement was born. Within two years there would be over 100,000 Scouts in the UK.

Scouts make a camp mattress.

Scouts cooking on fire.

A new movement

It should be remembered that Baden-Powell did not have a masterplan for the development of Scouting. All he was trying to do was to provide a scheme for existing organisations to use. The fact that Scouting established itself as its own youth movement was just as much of a surprise to him as it was to everyone else. In the months that followed, he was once again occupied with military matters, having accepted command of the Northumbria Division of the Territorial Army. But boys read the book, formed Patrols and Troops, and persuaded adults to become Scoutmasters. The true answer to the question 'Who started the Scouts?' is most probably 'the boys' rather than Baden-Powell himself.

The start of a movement

1908–1918

Humshaugh: the first Scout camp

If Baden-Powell wanted Brownsea Island to be kept low key, his next camping venture was just the opposite. This time, he wanted publicity. He wanted to show the world what could be done with a little imagination and enterprise.

Opportunity of a lifetime

The Humshaugh camp was announced in the first issue of *The Scout* on 18 April 1908. For the magazine's readers, the chance to camp with B-P seemed too good to be true. What was the catch? There was a competition, and an invitation to the camp was the prize. The 30 boys who had collected the most votes would be listed in the issue of *The Scout* published immediately before the camp.

A popularity contest?

The votes had little to do with democracy. Readers could vote for themselves, but only using the coupon in the magazine each week. Lists of the top fifty names were published weekly, encouraging people to keep voting. Baden-Powell may not have liked the concept behind the competition, but he did not own *The Scout*, so there was little he could do about it.

The intention was that Scouts could encourage friends to buy the magazine so that they could use their coupons. By the end of the competition, F.D. Watson had accumulated the most 'votes' – he appeared to have more than 29,000 friends, while the fiftieth boy in the league table had 5,350. The scheme must have attracted tens of thousands of sales by the time the camp was held at the end of August.

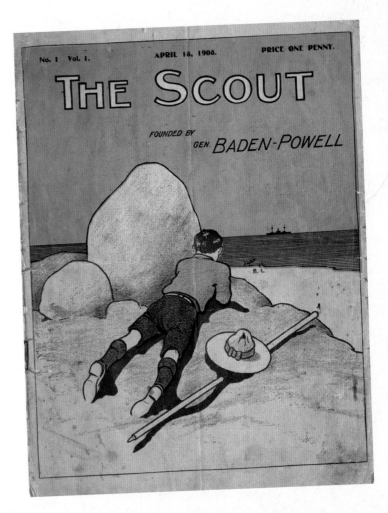

A late compromise

Baden-Powell was not impressed. In a letter to Keary, managing director of Pearsons Publishers, he wrote: 'There is something in it which I fear will put off some readers of the better sort.' Possibly to compensate for the magazine publisher's moneymaking scheme, Baden-Powell arranged for the first 20 unsuccessful boys to receive a Scout camera, and for the next 50 to receive a signed copy of *Scouting for Boys*.

In a last-minute compromise, Baden-Powell and Pearson agreed that an additional six boys could attend the camp. This Patrol was called the Wolves. The other five Patrols of six boys were named Kangaroos, Curlews, Ravens, Bulls and Owls. Perhaps regretting the way the selection had been handled, Baden-Powell wrote during the camp: 'I wish every Boy Scout in Britain could be with us here today.'

The location

The exact location of the camp was not revealed until the end of the competition, and for good reason: it had not yet been found. It was not until 9 August 1908 that Baden-Powell was able to write: 'I have arranged camping grounds thus: Camp at Walewick Grange five miles from Hexham (Station Chollerford) for a week, then Tramps to neighbouring spots and bivouacs for the nights.' The actual site was just south of a Roman wall, on a gently sloping hillside, adjacent to Carr Edge Plantations (grid reference NY 890697).

The camp opens

The Scout camp opened on 22 August 1908. Baden-Powell was unable to attend the opening as he had been called up for Territorial Army duties, but he arrived in time for the campfire that night.

Much of the food there came from local farms. Tents were also hired locally and Baden-Powell flew the same Union flag that he had used at Mafeking and Brownsea.

The programme

Monday 24 August – overcast and raining
Physical exercises led by W. Wakefield
Setting up of a loom in the woods and building a hut
Bivouac and straw mattress making
Making ration bags with needle and thread
Short game of football
How to make bread without yeast or chemicals
Campfire
Talk 'hints on tracking' by Pearse

Thursday 27 August – showers
P.E.
Changed position of tent
Played 'Scout meets Scout'
Patrol activities
First Aid instruction
Visit to Mr Chapman's home at Houxty; as it was wet the boys stayed over in the stables

Friday 28 August – cold and rain all day
Physical drill in saddle room
Stretcher drill
Tracking, whistles and hand signals
Chapman shows off his collection of 'Big Game' mounted trophies
Signalling practice
Tea, campfire, heard phonograph
At night Patrol Leaders went out rabbit shooting

Tuesday 1 September – heavy showers
Patrol Drill raising section tents as practice for sports day
Straw rope making
Badgework and 1st class tests
Debate in Bulls tent: 'Should rabbits be kept in tents?'
Evening lecture on kindness to animals

Thursday 3 September – overcast but dry
P.E.
Assist farmer with fence mending
Self-measurement as in Scouting for Boys
First Aid
Campfire for 1st class badge
March to Fourstones to take train to Newcastle-upon-Tyne to visit the Armstrong Whitworth Armoury Works at Elswick
Visited sail training ship 'Calliope' and a large crane
Campfire with Baden-Powell's yarns about Mafeking

Daily programme

6.30am	Turn out, air bedding; coffee and biscuit
7.00am	Physical exercises or instruction parade
7.30am	Stow tents and wash
8.00am	Prayers and flagbreak
8.30am	Breakfast
9.00am	Scouting practice
11.00am	Biscuit and milk
11.30am	Scouting games
1.30pm	Dinner
2.00pm	Rest (compulsory)
3.00pm	Scouting games
5.30pm	Tea
6.00pm	Recreation, camp games
7.30pm	Campfire
9.00pm	Biscuits and milk; turn in
9.30pm	Lights out

The 30 boys joined Baden-Powell in a daily 'flag breaking ceremony'. The flag is the same one that flew over Mafeking during B-P's time in South Africa.

Baden-Powell

A model for the future

In his final campfire address to the boys, B-P invoked the spirit of King Arthur and his Knights of the Round Table, who were associated with the area. 'You must never forget,' he said, 'that the distinguishing mark of a Scout should be his unselfishness. He should always think of others and try to help them before thinking of himself.'

The Humshaugh camp had been planned as a model, not just for those who had already joined the Scouts, but to show the world at large what Scouting was all about. Press coverage in the national newspapers brought the movement to wider attention.

But the best publicity was from the boys themselves. It was 'the very best holiday of my life,' said John Coats. 'I am sure every boy in the camp must wish to go there again next year.' They didn't – by next summer there was another idea for another type of a camp.

The first troops

During the first months of 1908, Patrols and Troops started by the Boys Brigade and the YMCA began to spring up in the UK. The appetite for the Scouts was well underway.

The first Troops

The first Scout Troops formed so quickly that it is impossible to know which was the very first.

Most registration details were stored locally, and in many cases, Troops were active long before anyone started filling in forms. At least 25 Scout Troops in the UK today have existed continuously since 1908.

Scouting spreads abroad

Within two years there were more than 100,000 Scouts in the UK and the movement had already spread abroad, first to the other parts of the British Empire – Australia, Canada, New Zealand, India and South Africa. In 1909, Chile was the first country outside of the British Empire to adopt Scouting. Manufacturers were also quick to cash in on the growing phenomena, producing toys and games with a Scouting theme, along with handbooks and fiction.

Gamages, a London department store, soon had a whole floor devoted to Scout equipment with its own shopping catalogue.

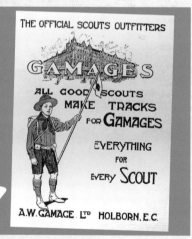

THE OFFICIAL SCOUTS OUTFITTERS

GAMAGES

ALL GOOD SCOUTS MAKE TRACKS FOR GAMAGES

EVERYTHING FOR EVERY SCOUT

A.W. GAMAGE LTD HOLBORN, E.C.

The first Bahamas Scout troop.

Getting organised

The lack of organisation at HQ threatened the reputation of the Scouts. So, in September 1908, Baden-Powell decided he needed a system to keep track of Scout Troops and Scoutmasters. Local advisory committees then asked all Patrols and Troops in their district to register, to appoint adults as Scoutmasters who were considered 'fit and proper', to award badges and to help the movement as best they could.

Two travelling inspectors were then appointed to help, advise and encourage – William Birkbeck for the north of England and Eric Walker for the south. All royalties from the bestselling Scouting for Boys were ploughed back in to funding the movement, its office and its growing staff. By 1909, the Scouts had acquired their first national headquarters building at 116–118 Victoria Street, London. Here, the paid staff worked hand-in-hand with the senior volunteers.

The 1st Saltburn Scout troop from North Yorkshire, UK, 1910.

Royal approval

Towards the end of the year, Baden-Powell was invited by King Edward VII to stay at Balmoral Castle in Scotland. During his visit, he was knighted for creating the Scout movement. The King agreed to review a rally of Scouts the following year, and the King's Scout Badge was introduced. The King also persuaded Baden-Powell to devote himself full-time to Scouting. This was what the movement needed.

As a souvenir of this historic visit, the King later sent Baden-Powell a small piece of venison bone mounted with a silver edge, bearing an inscription of a royal crown. The bone was all that remained of the joint of meat they had eaten together.

King Edward died in 1910, so King George V inspected the Scout rally in 1911.

35

Sea Scouts

Scouting was spreading across the UK, but Baden-Powell saw no reason why it should stop at the shores. Sea Scouting became an instantly popular branch of the movement and it remains so to this day.

As a young boy, Baden-Powell enjoyed boating holidays with his brothers. He once sailed a canvas boat up the River Thames over to the Rivers Severn and Wye. Their leader was his brother Warrington, who later achieved fame as a canoeist and, after a career at sea, became an expert in maritime law.

'Sea Scout Jones'

Baden-Powell wrote in Scouting for Boys that 'a Scout should be able to manage a boat, to bring it properly alongside a ship or pier'. Many Scout Troops had formed in the towns around Britain's coastline and rivers. In February 1909, The Scout reported: 'A new branch of Boy Scouts is springing up in Glasgow under the title of Sea Scouts. These Scouts will be just the same as Land Scouts [...] The only difference is that they will be trained on a naval basis, learning naval drills and visiting His Majesty's ships whenever possible.'

The Seamanship Badge was introduced in June 1909. A Scout who received it was then 'recognised by the rank of his badge' and could be referred to as 'Sea Scout Jones'.

A new manual

Baden-Powell wrote a small booklet on Sea Scouting for Boys in 1911. He later realised the need for a proper handbook and persuaded his brother Warrington to write one. Sea Scouting and Seamanship for Boys (1912) laid out a philosophy and training plan that prepared for Sea Scouting.

Sea camps

The Scout magazine ran another competition, this time for 100 Scouts to camp for a fortnight in August 1909 across two sites. A Troop of 50 'wet bobs' would sleep in hammocks on the ship Mercury, which was moored in the River Hamble at Buckler's Hard, Hampshire. The other 50 'land bobs' would camp nearby in the grounds of Lord Montague's estate at Beaulieu, Hampshire. Each Troop spent a week at each site.

Of the participants, 92 were the competition winners and the other eight were guests. Guests included B-P's nephew Donald, George Rodney and Humphrey Noble – who had camped at Brownsea and Humshaugh – along with the sons of Rudyard Kipling, Percy Everett and Lord Balfour. The camp was a great success.

Leysdown disaster

On 4 August 1912, nine Scouts drowned in an accident off the Isle of Sheppey. An ex-naval boat was carrying 23 Scouts from Walworth to their summer camp when a sudden storm caused the boat to capsize. A mass funeral service was held on 10 August, attended by thousands, including Scouts from many countries.

Another accident occurred the following year. The Daily Mirror had presented a 50-tonne ketch (small sailing boat) to the Sea Scouts, called the Mirror. The Mirror was hit by another vessel while at sea and four people lost their lives. In spite of these losses, the Sea Scouts kept going and thousands of its members have had naval careers.

Scouting for girls

> From the beginning, girls as well as boys were attracted to Scouting. Sisters did not wish to be left out when their brothers went off to play games and camp.

From his first pamphlet in 1907 outlining his scheme, Baden-Powell described Scouting as suitable for both girls and boys. In his early columns for *The Scout*, he encouraged girls to join, knowing they were as fit to be Scouts as boys. In 1909 *The Scout* and the *Headquarters Gazette* both listed Troops where girls were involved in Scouting.

However, attitudes of society of the time considered it absurd to involve girls in activities that were seen as the preserve of boys, and girls were discouraged from joining. To bridge this gap, in January 1909, Baden-Powell wrote in *The Scout* of the need to 'devise a scheme of Scouting better adapted' for girls.

A group of Girl Scouts, known to us as Kangaroo Patrol, created a Patrol magazine in May 1909. It was full of adventure stories with Scouts preventing robberies and kidnappings.

Maisie raised her staff straight up over her head and signed to Bonnie to halt.

D.H.W.R.1909.

Girl Guides

Baden-Powell chose the name 'Girl Guides', which was inspired by a corps of Indian guides 'distinguished for their general handiness and resourcefulness under difficulties... their keenness and courage... a force trained to take up any duties required on them, and to turn their hand to anything.' Symbolically, guides always know the way and can lead others.

Crystal Palace rally

On 4 September 1909, 10,000 Scouts gathered at Crystal Palace, London. This was the first big public appearance where Girl Scouts were included too.

When Baden-Powell was inspecting the Scouts, the Wolf Patrol of Girl Scouts introduced themselves to him. This public appearance was much photographed and commented on, demonstrating that the appetite for the Girl Guide movement was strong. The August 1909 edition of the Headquarters Gazette announced that a new scheme was being prepared for the 6,000 Girl Scouts that had already registered at HQ.

One of the Girl Scouts who attended the 'Boy Scout' rally at Crystal Palace in September 1909.

Handbook for Girl Guides

A booklet outlining the Girl Guides and their programme had been drafted for the movement's launch in 1910. It outlined the same aims of character development and citizenship training as Scouts, but with activities including 'home-making and mother-craft'. However, Baden-Powell insisted they would become equal partners to boys.

With his commitments to the Army and Scouts, Baden-Powell did not have time to run a second movement himself. He was delighted when his sister Agnes picked up the torch. She wrote a first handbook called *How Girls Can Help to Build the Empire*. This was followed in 1912 by the *Handbook for Girl Guides*: the foundation stone of the movement. Girls joined in their thousands, both in the UK and overseas.

The movement spread worldwide and by 1920, the Girl Guides were larger than the Scouts.

Introducing Olave

In January 1912, Baden-Powell met 23-year-old Olave St Clair Soames on the SS *Arcadian*, while sailing to America. Born in 1889 in Derbyshire, Olave was a great enthusiast for sports and outdoor living. The two shared a birthday: 22 February. Despite their age difference of 32 years, they had much in common. By the time the ship reached Jamaica the couple were secretly engaged. They married on 30 October at St Peter's Church near Poole in a simple ceremony attended by close relatives and friends. They were later given a Triumph Standard car from the Scouts, towards which 100,000 Scouts had each paid a penny.

Chief Guide

Olave took a great interest in the Scouts and ran her own Scout Troop. In 1915, she joined the Guides and quickly rose to County Commissioner for Sussex, then Chief Commissioner for England. Her relationship with Agnes Baden-Powell, who ran the Guides, was strained. In 1918, when a dispute occurred, B-P backed Olave to become Chief Guide, and his sister Agnes took a back seat. Together, Robert and Olave would devote themselves to travelling the world promoting the two great movements.

Robert, Olave and their three children lived in Pax Hill for more than 20 years.

Daily life with the Baden-Powells

Baden-Powell was very much a family man. Whenever possible Baden-Powell and Olave spent as much time as they could with their children.

After they married, Baden-Powell and Olave lived at Ewhurst Place in Sussex until 1917, when they rented a 15th-century farmhouse near Horley, Surrey. Their family grew, and after the war they bought Blackacre Farm in the picturesque village of Bentley in Hampshire. To mark the end of the war, they changed the name of the house to Pax Hill, where they lived for more than 20 years with their children Peter, Heather and Betty, playing with them in the garden or picnicking on the riverbanks nearby. Each child learned to ride horses and they had a large collection of pet dogs, rabbits and pigeons.

Morning routine

Baden-Powell usually rose at about 5am, a habit from his days spent in the Army in India. This allowed him a couple of hours to work without interruption. After a cup of tea he would paint for a while until 7.30am. Then, he and Olave would walk the dogs, and they would breakfast with the family and any guests. In this way, he estimated that he crammed 'thirteen months of life into each year instead of twelve'.

Mountains of mail

Baden-Powell employed a secretary, Eileen Wade, who lived in a nearby cottage. She helped him with the daily mountain of mail. Letters could be from former Army colleague, asking for work, from the Girl Scouts in America asking his opinion on a memorial or from a magazine requesting an article. And, of course, Olave received her own large bag of mail too.

In the afternoon B-P tended to the garden and walked the dogs. Then it was time for tea: the main occasion when the family would gather. Guests were always welcome at Pax Hill – from distinguished visitors to campers who pitched their tents in the front garden. The garden at Pax Hill was a source of pleasure and visitors often found themselves trimming hedges or pruning roses. In the evening, Baden-Powell would often show films that he had made himself of his tours.

Thrifty household

Baden-Powell made no money from Scouting. He wrote to supplement his Army pension. But they were a family of simple needs. B-P's journeys both around the UK and overseas were not funded by the Scouts. He wrote articles for every issue of the *Headquarters Gazette* (later called *The Scouter*) and *The Scout*, compilations of which were republished as books such as *Adventures and Accidents* (1934) and *Scouting Round the World* (1935).

Winding down

A sketchbook was Baden-Powell's constant companion. He quickly sketched whatever caught his eye. He would later work up some of these sketches into finished pieces. His other passion was fishing. When he needed some space, he would go off for a few days with his rods and tackle. He only fished for sport, returning anything he caught to the river. Olave loved to play tennis and hockey, and she set up a team made up of family and servants to play other teams in the local villages.

Wolf Cubs

The growth of Scouting led to demand from younger children who wanted to join in the fun. The movement had been designed for those aged 11 and over, but of course, younger siblings could not wait.

Younger Scouts

When younger children turned up to Troop meetings they would not always be turned away. Scouting couldn't be 'watered down' for them, so unofficial junior Troops existed as early as 1909.

From 1914, the junior Scouts, known as Wolf Cubs, had their own uniform of a dark green cap with yellow cord border and either a dark green or blue jersey. The younger boys were taught simple knots, Scout tracking signs, basic semaphore and rudimentary First Aid. The more advanced activities, such as Morse code and stretcher drill, would be the reserve of Scouts. But camping was the thing the youngsters craved.

Learning First Aid was an important skill.

All change

At the outbreak of World War One in 1914, things changed. Older Scouts and Scoutmasters joined the Army and women then moved into roles formerly held by men. Younger boys were desperate to join in with Scouting just like their brothers.

A well-organised junior Scout section would fulfil several needs at once. Helped by Vera Barclay, Baden-Powell threw himself into the structure and philosophy of the new section. Wolf Cubs had proved to be highly successful, with more than 10,000 people registering within the first year. These early packs fed helpful information back to HQ. The section officially launched in December 1916.

Wolves in the jungle

Baden-Powell understood the importance of imaginative games for younger children. He chose the title 'Wolf Cubs' as the name 'wolf' was the Native American word for a good scout. The wolf theme inspired him to ask his friend, Rudyard Kipling, to allow *The Jungle Books* to be used as an imaginative setting for his new section. *The Jungle Books* had been popular with younger children since their first publication in 1894.

Cubs learnt to communicate using semaphore.

This storybook backdrop was the perfect way to introduce youngsters to the disciplines of Scouting while having fun: just like Mowgli, who was guided through the jungle by wise animals.

What Baden-Powell did with Kipling's text reveals a great deal about both men's characters. B-P wanted the boys to be inspired to adventure and to act as a Pack to develop teamwork, whereas Kipling focused on Mowgli, the unique individual who would come to lead the Pack.

The Wolf Cub's Handbook

Baden-Powell re-interpreted the stories from *The Jungle Book* for the Cubs in his own language, with a Scouting moral attached.

The Wolf Cub's Handbook was published from 1916 until 1966, with 16 editions. It was divided into wolfish 'Bites', each one being a combination of a jungle story, new games and jungle dances. This introduction appeared in every edition:

'Every boy, like every young Wolf, has a hearty appetite. This book is a meal offered by an old Wolf to the young Cubs. There is juicy meat in it to be eaten, and there are tough bones to be gnawed. But if every Cub who devours it will tackle the bone as well as the meat, and will eat up the fat with the lean, I hope that he will get good strength, as well as some enjoyment, out of every bite. B-P'

Cheery Cubs learning to knit in 1916.

JUNGLE LAND

The Grand Howl

Cubs were required to know the Grand Howl, the Wolf Cub salute and the Wolf Cub Promise and Law. Their salute was symbolic of the two ears of the wolf and there were two parts to the Law:

'The Cub gives into the Old Wolf,
'The Cub does not give in to himself.'

The Promise was a simplified version of the Scout Promise, without the words 'On my honour'. 'Do Your Best' became the Cub Motto, which is where the phrase 'dyb dyb dyb' ('Do Your Best') and 'dob dob dob' (Do Our Best) came from. This originally accompanied the Grand Howl at the formal opening and closing of every Pack meeting.

There was a new programme of 12 badges specially designed for Cubs. Initially, there was no handbook or specific training for leaders, however, the principle suggested by B-P would be equally applicable today:

'We teach them small things in play which will eventually fit them for doing big things in earnest.'

Whether Kipling approved of his books being used in this way has been a matter of debate over the years. Baden-Powell had invited Kipling to the launch of the Wolf Cubs and of *The Wolf Cub's Handbook* in 1916, and Kipling's response shows his affection, admiration and enthusiasm for Baden-Powell and Scouting. This can perhaps be seen as a good conclusion to the debate.

December 1916

Bateman's
Burwash
Sussex

Dear Baden-Powell,

I'm afraid I can't be up on Saturday much as I should like to see your Wolf Cubs. The more I see what the whole Scout movement has done and is doing in this world, and the more I realise what the great mass of youth might not have done if it had been left undirected, the more impressed I am with the immense value of your work. The only thing I can compare it to is what the Salvation Army did years back. You ought to be a happy man these days.

Yours sincerely
Rudyard Kipling

Vera Barclay and the Wolf Cubs

Vera Barclay was a pioneer for women in Scouting. She was not only one of the first 'Lady Scoutmasters', but also developed a varied programme for the Wolf Cubs and encouraged other women to become involved.

Early life

Vera Charlesworth Barclay was born in 1893 and grew up in a large family based in Hertford Heath, north of London, where her father was a vicar. In 1912, at the age of 19, she worked with the Scout Troop in her village, joining a small but growing number of women in the Scout movement.

Over the next eight years, she would heavily influence the Cubs and Scouts. She would become one of the first woman to hold a post in the masculine environment that was the early Scout Headquarters.

Keen youngsters

As soon as Scouting began there was a clamouring of younger voices wanting to join in too, but they were too young. Vera witnessed the demand first-hand. She described trying to let the boys down gently:

'Often as I walked through the village, one or another of these keen-eyed, neglected youngsters would run after me, calling, "Miss, miss! If yer wants anuver Scout, I'm ready!" "Right," I would answer, "I'll certainly remember you," and I would officially take his name and send him along with rekindled hope. But two years is terribly long when you are nine.'

First Wolf Cub Packs

In January 1914, the *Headquarters Gazette* published an article called 'Wolf Cubs or Young Scouts – How to train them', summarising the new section and its rules. Vera was finally able to keep her promise to the boys who had been desperate to join her Scout Troop: she started the 1st Hertford Heath Wolf Cub Pack and her sister Angela became Lady Cubmaster. They ran a programme packed with imaginative games designed to appeal to the younger boys. This closely echoed Baden-Powell's ideas for Wolf Cubs, which were still evolving.

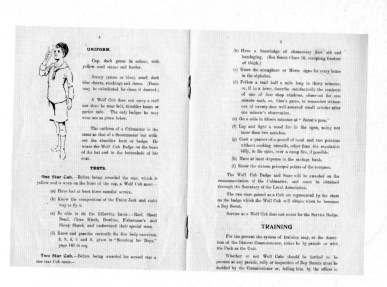

Women in Scouting

Vera was a strong and early advocate for the involvement of women in Scouting. When discussing how a Pack should be run, she stated:

'There should be a separate Cubmaster... Boys under the age of eleven will get on quite as well (perhaps better) in the charge of a woman Cubmaster – provided she is the right sort... If every Scoutmaster could persuade a woman of his acquaintance to run a Pack in connection with his Troop, he would find Scouting in the future vastly simplified.'

Vera and Angela Barclay were amongst the first Cubmasters to receive their warrants, and their names appeared in the first list of Cubmasters in the December 1914 *Headquarters Gazette*. In January 1915, Vera published an article in the *Headquarters Gazette* entitled 'How a Lady can Train the Cubs'.

A job at HQ

Along with many other women of her generation, World War One changed Vera's life, and with that came a range of new experiences. In 1916 she was a nurse in a Red Cross Hospital on the south coast. Just as the Somme Offensive was launched in July 1916, she received a letter from Percy Everett offering her a job at Scout Headquarters. In her reply, she said:

'You can imagine how awfully surprised I was at being offered a "staff job" at Headquarters! [...] If you and the Chief think I should be any good of course I am delighted to accept. I can at all counts "do my best"!'

Her eagerness to start work was clear. She was entering a male-dominated world. For a 23-year-old woman whose upper middle-class upbringing would have not prepared her for a career, this would have been quite an undertaking.

The Handbook

The *Wolf Cubs Handbook* was launched on 29 November 1916, just in time for Christmas. Vera claimed that 'the dullest and sleepiest little Cub could not help but be inflamed by it'; it was full of 'fascinating games' and new ideas. Vera worked closely with Baden-Powell and heavily influenced the content of the Handbook.

Wolf Cub badges

Vera wrote the criteria for the original 12 Wolf Cub badges, and by August 1916, 'The Cubmaster's Page' appeared in the *Headquarters Gazette*, written by Vera. Over the next four years, this was the main source of news on the Wolf Cubs. Vera drew on her experiences to give practical help and ideas on the Cub programme.

In October 1916, Baden-Powell made the Cubs official members of the Scout movement. This brought some changes to the Wolf Cubs programme. To attain their first and second stars, Wolf Cubs were now required to turn a somersault!

This caused some concern as Cubmasters discussed what defined a somersault. Vera reassured them that their Cubs were not being encouraged to perform Olympic-standard tumbles consisting of 'jumping in the air from a standing position, turning over in the air and coming down to a standing position again ... the ordinary head-over-heels performance of small boys is the recognised and official test!'

Artist Badge

Collector Badge

Athlete Badge

House Orderly Badge

First Aider Badge

Woodworker Badge

Guide Badge

Signaller Badge

Swimmer Badge

Observer Badge

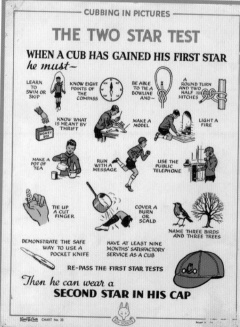

Weaver Badge

Team Player Badge

Launch of the Wolf Cubs

On 16 December 1916, the newly revamped Wolf Cubs were given a formal launch at Caxton Hall in London, which it is likely that Vera planned as a part of her role.

The event had included a speech by Baden-Powell, a Grand Howl led by the 11th East Ham Pack, the investiture of a new Cub into the 11th East Ham Pack and displays given by local Packs, including of the controversial somersault and knitting.

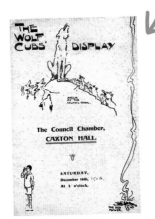

Wolf Cubs demonstrating the controversial somersault.

Wolf Cub advisor

Following the launch of the Wolf Cubs, Vera advised Cub Leaders on how to persuade parents of the value of the movement. She suggested that leaders should hold meetings for parents to ask questions and observe activities. These meetings still take place today.

Vera travelled the country visiting Packs and events, and in her monthly column she listed the places she had visited. A new magazine called *The Wolf Cub* launched in December 1916, in which Vera and the team created content aimed at Cubs themselves.

Silver Wolf

Vera organised for the Cubs to be involved in the first international jamboree, and was afterwards presented with the Silver Wolf award in recognition of her efforts. Vera had been promoted to Cub Secretary in acknowledgement of her tremendous work and high level of responsibility. She then developed additional resources for Cub Leaders, and in June 1920 she published *The Book of Cub Games*, quickly followed by *Character Training in the Wolf Cub Pack* and *Stories of the Saints by Candlelight*.

'I must say goodbye'

In her Cubmaster's Page in September 1920, Vera reflected on the four years since she took up her Scout post. She wrote the article 'A History of Cubbing' marking the key moments in the section's development. She then wrote 'the most difficult bit of the Cubmaster's Page I have ever had to write', where she announced that she was leaving the Association to become a Sister of Charity of St Vincent de Paul.

When Vera had begun her role at Headquarters on 6 September 1916, she had challenged the watered-down version of the Cub programme in January 1914, and had been instrumental in creating a fun, imaginative programme for younger boys to develop life skills. By the time she relinquished her role, she was leaving a Movement 'full of Cub experts who can write, speak and organise'.

Vera did not work for the charity for long and continued to be active in Scouting. She attended an early Akela training course at Gilwell Park, wrote a stream of books on Scout and Cub techniques and a raft of children's fiction. She died in 1989 at the age of 95. The Scout tracking symbol for 'gone home' – the dot in a circle – appears on her grave.

Scouts in World War One

As a former soldier, Baden-Powell took a huge interest in the Great War, as it was then known. He was faced with a dilemma: how could his new movement make the most effective contribution to the war effort while remaining committed to peace?

Be prepared

David Lloyd George, prime minister of Britain, wrote in 1917: 'It is no small matter to be proud of that the Association was able within a month of the outbreak of war to give the most energetic and intelligent help in all kinds of service.'

Praise indeed, but at the outset of the war, the Scouts were anything but prepared. War threatened the existence of Scouting, and large numbers of adult leaders would be called to serve their country. Baden-Powell did not welcome the war. Government ministers intended to militarise youth organisations, including the Scouts, but Baden-Powell refused this. Despite his reservations about the war and its impact on Scouting, just before war was declared on 4 August, Baden-Powell offered the services of the movement to the government. The government gratefully accepted.

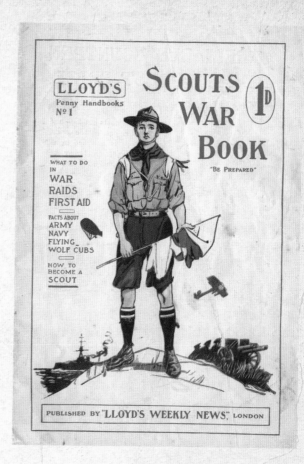

Baden-Powell's role

Baden-Powell wanted an active, front line role, but he was a retired cavalry solider aged 57, so Lord Kitchener, the Secretary for War, said no. Kitchener said that only one of the country's retired generals could have mobilised the nation's youth. Volunteer battalions from other youth organisations were sent to fight, such as the Church Lads Brigade, ut Kitchener was against a Scout battalion.

Scout Defence Corps

This did not deter Baden-Powell. In November 1914's *Headquarters Gazette*, he announced his plans for a scheme for Scouts aged 16 and 17 years of age: the

Scout Defence Corps. Fearing invasion, he wrote: 'A boy of 16 trained in discipline and marksmanship will be worth a dozen trained to nothing in particular.'

Membership was voluntary and the Corps would not be a permanent feature of Scouting. To pre-empt inevitable criticism, he added, 'It is not militarism but a struggle against militarism.'

He wrote a small book, *Marksmanship for Boys*, to support the scheme, but it was not popular. The Corps failed to secure Home Office recognition. Usual Scout Troop activities suffered as the Corps Scouts could not devote the time to their normal training. Retaining Scouts soon became a major problem.

Hospital help

As honorary Colonel, Baden-Powell was invited to visit his two old regiments on duty in France in 1915. While he enjoyed being back in uniform and among fellow soldiers for ten days, he also witnessed for himself the carnage first-hand, and it shocked him.

But the trip did allow him to visit some of the hospitals and YMCA recreation huts that had been established. More were needed, in Baden-Powell's eyes, to improve the welfare and morale of the soldiers. He came away impressed and determined: here was a cause through which Scouting could make a valuable contribution directly to the war effort.

As well as issuing a fundraising appeal to the movement, he approached the Mercers Company, one of the ancient City of London trade guilds, which Baden-Powell was involved with. The Mercers funded the first and largest of six Scout huts and, later on, another hut and a marquee.

Scouts in France

The 'Mercers Arms' hut opened near Calais on 21 July 1915, with a Troop of French Scouts forming a guard of honour. It was staffed by Scouters in their uniform who had responded to appeals in the *Headquarters Gazette*, provided they were unfit or not the correct age for military service. Another hut, this time funded by the Scouts, was opened by Olave at Etaples in December that same year. It cost over £1,000 but could accommodate 1,000 men. Both Baden-Powell and Olave worked serving tea and attending to the men themselves. Scouts also raised funds to buy and equip ambulances for the western front.

Eventually, Baden-Powell spent so much time in France during the war that the Germans were suspicious he was spying. This was not true, but the British government did not deny the rumours. In fact, Baden-Powell added to the confusion by publishing two books, *Quick Training for War* (1914), which sold 65,000 copies in the first month, followed by *My Adventures as a Spy* (1915).

Huts such as this one at Etaples provided soldiers with a place to relax as they spent time away from the Front.

DESIGNED BY LT. GEN. SIR R. S. S. BADEN POWELL.

Are **YOU** in this?

PUBLISHED BY THE PARLIAMENTARY RECRUITING COMMITTEE, LONDON.—POSTER NO.112.   PRINTED BY JOHNSON, RIDDLE & CO., LTD., LONDON, S.E.

This recruitment poster, designed by Baden-Powell, shows various ways people could contribute to the war effort. In the centre, a Scout hands a message to a soldier.

Scouts on the home front

By 1914, the Scouts had been running for five years. Boys and young men had gained useful skills, from field-craft and camp cooking to signalling and sailing. Skills which, as World War One broke out, could be put to very good use.

Doing their bit

Many older Scouts and their leaders joined the Armed Forces, but Baden-Powell felt that the younger Scouts could also 'do their bit' by supporting services at home. They played a crucial role in supporting the war effort with non-military work.

Scouts turned their hands to all manner of tasks. They acted as messengers at railway stations, police stations, at Post Offices and even at the War Office. One of the early skills a Scout developed was First Aid. Scouts were asked to help care for the sick and injured men in the Armed Forces, as well as civilians caught up in attacks. They carried out police work, with each Troop reporting to the Chief Police Constable in their county.

They came under fire at Whitby, Scarborough and Hartlepool where they were guarding telegraph wires and guarding the coasts. They worked day and night. Some were even involved behind the front line in France, moving ammunitions.

Guarding the shores

One of the first roles that Scouts undertook was supporting the Coastguard. The fear of invasion by Germany was a very real threat, so watching the coast, ports and estuaries was crucial. As early as 7 August 1914, the Admiralty had requested the immediate service of 1,000 Scouts to assist Coastguards on the east coast. Eventually, 23,000 Scouts would be involved in this line of work alone.

Scouts were supervised by the Coastguard but remained under the orders of their Patrol Leaders. Their activities included coast watching, sending signals and delivering messages. They were responsible for their own activities and actions, so this was a practical example of one of Scouting's core principles: giving boys independence. The Scouts received a basic subsistence allowance for their work. Some Scout groups guarded railway junctions and telegraph and telephone cables against sabotage.

Coast Watching by Ernest Stafford Carlos (1915) shows the crucial role Sea Scouts were playing on the Home Front. Their binoculars and semaphore flags are ready for action.

Scouts guarding railway points against enemy sabotage.

A Sea Scout demonstrating his signalling skills using semaphore flags. This knowledge would prove very helpful while supporting the Coastguard.

Working the land

Many Scouts volunteered to work on farms during harvest time. At this time, most farm work was done by hand. As men left farms to join the Armed Forces, Scouts took on some of the farm work. The St Luke's Mission Troop from Chelsea adapted their summer camp into a working farm holiday.

Food wasn't the only resource that needed to be grown. Flax was an important crop and was used to make a tough, canvas-like cloth. This was then made into everything from tents to aircraft wing covers.

In August 1914, rural France was preparing for the harvest, but many farm workers had been called up to fight. If the harvest crops were not gathered, the country would face serious food shortages. France issued an appeal across the channel for help with the harvest.

Scouts helping to gather the flax harvest.

Working on a farm released farm workers for service with the Armed Services.

> I am thirteen, and big for my age.
> I should be pleased to hear from you as I am most desirous of going.
>
> Yours Faithfully
> Rex Stent

185375
ack 26/8/14 (46)

AUG 1914 13 St., John's Villas
Highgate.
August 23rd 1914

Dear Sir
I saw by an article in the "Daily Mail" that Boy Scouts are required for the harvest fields.
I belong to the 1st North London Lord Kitchener's Troop.

In the early days of the war, Scout Headquarters were flooded by letters from Scouts wanting to know how they could help with the war effort.

Every penny counts

The Scout Hut and Ambulance Fund came about during this time. As today, Scouts during the war came up with some innovative ways of raising money. One Cub Pack spent a whole day collecting acorns, which were useful for animal feed, and sold them. The Scouts of Belfast raised more than £600 by selling bottles. Much-needed ambulances were purchased with the funds, which ended up in service as far afield as the Middle East.

Pedal power

The role of messenger boy was very important in a time before mass telecommunications. In 1914, few homes or public buildings had telephones. Telegrams and letters were the main methods of communication and they had to be delivered by hand.

Messenger boys were stationed at government offices, police stations and other buildings. The messenger boy needed to be healthy, strong, reliable and have a good sense of direction, criteria that many Scouts fulfilled.

Teams of Scout messengers took turns for 'duty' at key locations such as police stations.

Wolf Cubs on the home front

The Wolf Cub movement was formalised in 1916, during the darkest days of the war. By 1918, more than 37,000 boys had joined the section. The movement may owe some of this success to the unprecedented numbers of women who took up jobs on the Home Front, many of whom were mothers. Cubs would have been a perfect activity to keep boys occupied and safe after school!

Cubs helped by knitting items for troops and stuffing pillows with newspaper. They also learnt skills that would enable them to help out around the home, including peeling vegetables, cleaning shoes and basic housework, no doubt a great help for working mums.

Recovery and remembrance

By the end of the war, the Scouts had made an outstanding contribution both on the Home Front and in the Armed Forces. It was a contribution that was recognised at the highest level. David Lloyd George, British Prime Minister, stated:

'When the boyhood of a nation can give such practical proofs of its honour, straightness and loyalty there is not much danger of that nation going under, for these boys are in training to render service to their country as leaders in all walks of life in the future.'

The Scouts did not come through the war unscathed. It is estimated that 250,000 members of the Scout movement in Britain went to fight for 'King and country'. It is also estimated that 7,000 did not return. Many now lie in war graves. Fifteen Scouts were decorated with the Victoria Cross for their courage.

The experiences gained by the Scouts who had undertaken war work meant that there was a new generation of leaders ready to rebuild the movement.

A global effort

Scouts all over the world contributed to the war effort. Here are just a few examples of the ways that Scouts served their communities and defended their freedoms.

'Every Scout to Feed a Soldier'

USA

In the United States, Scouts were quick to rally behind the war effort. In 1917, as the USA entered the war, Scouts were encouraged to plant vegetable gardens under the slogan 'Every Scout to Feed a Soldier'. As many as 12,000 Scout farms sprung up.

Working with the US Navy, Scout coastal patrols began guarding the nation's shores while the organisation also pledged aid to the American Red Cross. Other duties involved distributing literature – over 300 million items were delivered by Scouts – and conserving supplies of food and fuel. American Scouts also made a significant financial contribution, selling 2,350,977 Liberty Loan bonds, totalling $147,876,902. They also sold war savings stamps, to a value of $53,043,698.

By the end of World War One, Scouts had proved themselves a loyal and efficient force for good. Working now under the slogan: 'The War Is Over, But Our Work Is Not', Scouts continued to serve their communities, most notably during the influenza epidemic that followed the war.

Scouts defend their freedom

Ukraine

The first Scout Troops formed in Western Ukraine in 1911 and were well established in 1913 – the eve of World War One. The war led to the collapse of the two powers occupying the Ukrainian territory, the Austro-Hungarian monarchy and tsarist Russia, which inevitably threw the fledgling movement into turmoil.

Hundreds of boys who were involved with Scouting volunteered to join the armed forces to defend their country's freedom. Although forgoing any hope of normal Scouting, they did help bring about formation of the Ukrainian National Republic in 1918

Sacrifice and propaganda

Canada

In Ottawa, Canada, Boy Scouts responded to the call of God and Country by forming the Headquarters' Patriotic Relief. In 1914, they took to the streets in support of the war, wearing their uniforms, accompanied by bagpipers, flags, drums and bugles.

They were quite literally drumming up public support. The hope was that the conflict would end quickly and decisively, but as the war progressed, it became clear that the human cost would be much greater than anticipated and the country suffered heavy casualties. Thousand of former Scouts lost their lives.

The Scout War Memorial in Oxshott, Kingston upon Thames, UK, was erected in memory of the 70 members of that district who were killed during World War One.

Jack Cornwell

> **The actions of an ordinary boy in extraordinary circumstances led to a new award: the Cornwell Badge. This is still awarded to Scouts under the age of 25 who show courage.**

Early life

John Travers 'Jack' Cornwell was known simply as Jack. Born in Leyton, London, on 8 January 1900, like many boys his age Jack became a keen Scout. 'Nothing was too hard for him... he would attempt any task,' his Scoutmaster, J.F. Avery, recalled. He was was one of five siblings. Cornwell left school and became a delivery boy. Then, on 21 July 1915, he walked into a local Navy recruitment office armed with good references and enlisted.

Just months later, on 1 May 1916, he officially passed out as Boy Seaman, First Class, J.T. Cornwell J/42563.

Cornwell was then ordered to join HMS Chester at Rosyth, Scotland, which was about to embark on its maiden voyage. But by 30 May, the Chester was needed for battle and was diverted to the Danish coast. The Battle of Jutland was about to begin: a battle that would change the face of sea warfare forever.

The Battle of Jutland

On 31 May the German fleet was spotted. The men on lookout heard distant gunfire and the ship was put on 'Action Stations'. Jack's job was to stand by his gun and take orders through his headphones. He alone was responsible for setting his gun's sights, making sure it hit its target.

From out of the mist, four enemy ships appeared. They concentrated their fire on the Chester and the ship was hit 17 times with large shells. Jack's gun was one of the first to be knocked out, before he had a chance to use it. He was surrounded by devastation as his comrades lay around him, dead and injured. Jack had received a mortal wound himself, but he stood at his post until the ship was eventually relieved by the rest of the fleet.

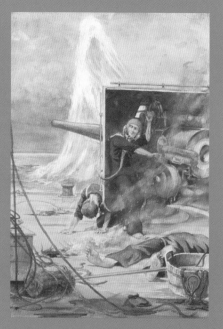

HMS Chester finally returned to Immingham, Lincolnshire, where the wounded were taken to Grimsby hospital. Jack was told that nothing could be done for him. Admiralty Surgeon D.C.S. Stephenson attended to him and found him to be extremely brave when he received this news. Jack died in the hospital on 2 June 1916, aged just 16 years and 6 months.

Private grief

This was the first and only full-scale engagement of the British and German fleets in World War One. The British lost 14 ships and 6,784 lives while the Germans lost 11 ships and 3,058 lives. HMS Chester lost 35 lives, six of them only boys. As word spread of these losses, the nation's morale sank.

Jack's captain wrote to Lily Cornwell, his mother, saying: 'He remained steady at his most exposed post at the gun, waiting for orders... But he felt he might be needed, and, indeed, he might have been; so he stayed there standing and waiting, under heavy fire, with just his own brave heart and God's help to support him.'

His mother arranged for a private funeral and he was buried in a shared grave in Manor Park Cemetery. Lily perhaps didn't realise that the Navy would pay for a private grave and funeral, or perhaps she had preferred to avoid a formal, public event. Her grief was not allowed to remain private for long.

A national hero

The story of Jack's bravery had captured the public imagination. The second year of the war was drawing to a close and news was not positive. The act of this ordinary boy became headlines and there was public outrage that this national hero did not have his own grave. On 29 July 1916, Jack was reburied with full military honours in a private grave at Manor Park Cemetery. The funeral was preceded by a spectacular procession with hundreds of Scouts lining the route.

Victoria Cross

On 15 September the London Gazette announced: 'The King has been graciously pleased to approve the grant of the Victoria Cross to Boy Seaman, First Class, John Travers Cornwell ONJ 42563 (died 2 June 1916), for the conspicuous act of bravery specified below:

'Mortally wounded early in the action, Boy Seaman, First Class, John Travers Cornwell remained standing alone at the most exposed post, quietly awaiting orders, until the end of the action, with the gun's crew dead and wounded all around him.'

King George V endorsed the award and Lily Cornwell was invited to Buckingham Palace to receive the Victoria Cross on behalf of her son. Jack's was one of four Victoria Crosses awarded at the Battle of Jutland. Baden-Powell also paid tribute to the boy's heroism. In the September edition of the Headquarters Gazette, the Cornwell Badge for bravery was announced. It exists to this day.

An elaborate monument was erected over Jack Cornwell's grave. By the end of 1916 his father was buried here too, and his mother in 1919. This image was taken in 1934.

Photo, Elliott & Fry

Roland Philipps

Roland Philipps was one of Scouting's most charismatic and influential early leaders. Despite being involved with Scouting for just five years, Roland made an outstanding contribution that continues to be felt today.

Roland supported the development of early Scouting in east London, where he held the title of East London Commissioner. He wrote Scouting manuals and organised the Hackney Scout Lectures, each of which was attended by up to 700 enthusiastic Scouts.

He encouraged young people to develop new skills and take on leadership roles. He was only a few years older than the Scouts, so he knew how to engage his audience. Roland became something of a hero to his band of loyal followers.

Peace versus war

Roland wished to serve his country but struggled to reconcile these feelings with his Scout values of peace and friendship. Following the outbreak of World War One Roland became a Lieutenant in the 9th Battalion, Royal Fusiliers. Before leaving for the Western Front Roland purchased a house in Stepney and wrote to Baden-Powell expressing his wishes:

'In case during the war I go on the bigger Scouting expedition, as so many have already done, I want to ask you as a special kindness to pass over the buildings, on my behalf, to the Scouts I care for so greatly in East London. One could live or die gladly in this or any other world if one knew that Scout ideas were held on high by the men and boys of this country.'

Injured in action

On 3 July 1916, Roland was injured during the Battle of the Somme. His trench was hit, which opened an old wound. He refused to leave the front line, and on 7 July, led his men out of the trench. Roland was then tragically shot in the head. He was just 26 years old.

The Scouting community mourned his loss. A memorial parade was held two weeks later. Thousands of Scouts made their way through east London. Roland's grave was marked with a fleur-de-lis and the tracking symbol for 'gone home'.

One of the very popular Scouting manuals written by Roland.

Roland wearing his Scout uniform with pride.

Roland's legacy

Roland's house provided a headquarters for east London Scouts for more than 60 years. When it was eventually sold, funds were used to buy the present-day headquarters, which was named the Roland Philipps Scout Centre.

At the same time, a fund was set up to support Scouts from east London, assisting with the cost of attending camps and other Scout adventures. Roland's family crest appears on the scarf of the East London District Scouts, ensuring he is still remembered in the area he gave so much to.

Between the wars

1919–1938

Gilwell Park

Known throughout the world as the home of Scouting, Gilwell Park is a country estate that has been owned by the Scouts since 1919. Over the years, thousands of people of every nationality have camped and trained here.

B-P's training school

In 1918, as the war was coming to a close, Baden-Powell expressed his wish to establish a training school for leaders and also to provide a campsite for the Scouts of east London. William de Bois Maclaren, a wealthy Scottish businessman, had offered to pay for a site. P.B. Nevill, Commissioner for East London and the Warden of Roland House, had been tasked with finding a site. He wrote:

'... Maclaren dined with me at Roland House on 29 November 1918. This was at the request of B-P who sent him to me as he wanted to give a camping ground for the boys of east London. He said "you find what you want and I will buy it". I told him that what I wanted was a site adjoining Epping or Hainault Forest and I spent every available weekend on my motorbike touring the area trying to find somewhere.'

A derelict estate

Gilwell Park was discovered thanks to a tip from local Assistant Scout Leader and bird-watcher, John Gayfer. It was a derelict 55-acre estate that had been empty for fifteen years. Its last owner was a Victorian inventor, manufacturer and poet called William Gibbs who created Gibbs' toothpaste. He died in 1900 and his descendants lived on the estate for some years afterwards. Nevill continued: 'I went to Gilwell on Saturday, 8 March 1919. I did not know the extent of the estate at the time but I found the old notice board advertising its sale on the ground behind a hedge and from this I managed to get the agent's name.'

The vision becomes a reality

While on an American lecture tour, Baden-Powell received a telegram about the discovery. He told Nevill to purchase it if he thought the place was right, and on his return, he visited immediately to see it for himself.

His secretary, Eileen Wade, accompanied him and recalled in her autobiography how, despite the pouring rain, his face lit up when he realised that his dream for a home for Scouting, where his vision could be lived out, was to become a reality at last.

The opening ceremony

Gilwell Park was purchased for £7,000 and Maclaren donated a further £3,000 to help restore the White House. Gilwell's official opening ceremony was held on 26 July 1919, with a rally of 700 Scouts. Maclaren's wife cut ribbons in the Scout colours of green and yellow, and Baden-Powell presented Maclaren with the movement's highest award for good service, the Silver Wolf.

Although this house was never Baden-Powell's home, he visited frequently. He would camp or sleep in a caravan. The place meant so much to him that it became the 'home of Scouting'.

Guests at the opening rally, 26 July 1919.

The first Scouts at Gilwell Park

Negotiations to purchase the estate commenced, and by Easter 1919 Scouts started clearing up the place. On the Thursday before Easter, a small group of Nevill's East London Rovers became the first Scout campers at Gilwell. Arriving in the rain, they spent their first night sleeping inside an old wooden shed, which is now known at the Pigsty and has been preserved as a monument to these pioneers!

In 1919, Scouting had gone from strength to strength and had more than 205,000 youth members. Not all of these young people were able to get the most out of Scouting though, due to a lack of both facilities and leaders. The first leaders' training course ran in September 1919, overlooked by an enormous oak tree that is now known throughout the world. This event continues to be commemorated every year by a 'Reunion' held to celebrate the contribution of the 160,000 Scouting volunteers active in the UK today

Scout Leaders taking a few minutes to relax while on the pilot Wood Badge course, September 1919.

Leadership training

The training methods for Scout Leaders that were developed at Gilwell Park are today emulated worldwide, and many leaders from around the world have trained here. The site has been enhanced by many structures and buildings of significance to the Scouting world, including signposts showing directions to every World Scout Jamboree. Former Scouts have often deposited their memoirs and log books at Gilwell Park for safe-keeping and future use. Gilwell Park now houses The Scouts Heritage Collection, which has amassed around 250,000 items, from letters and photographs to uniform and memorabilia – and even Baden-Powell's caravan.

During the pilot Wood Badge course one of the practical challenges was to build a trestle bridge.

12th Epping Forest raising fallen fruit trees on the Gilwell estate, May 1919.

12th Epping Troop carrying out cooking tests, May 1919.

The first female leaders to benefit from training at Gilwell Park attended the inaugural Cub training course in May 1921. In recognition of the number of women working with the Scouts section, a specific training offer was developed for them and the first course was held in February 1924.

The White House today

The White House sits at the centre of Gilwell Park. Records show that buildings have been on the site since 1407. Osborne Hall occupied the spot in the 1430s, and was demolished in 1754 by William Skirmshire to make way for the current building. Later owners added the rare crinoline staircase, built to accommodate the fashionable wide skirts of the mid-19th century. In 1771, the property was bought by Leonard Tresilian. It then passed to his daughter Margaret and her husband William Bassett Chinnery. They had three children there and the house became their family home.

The White House is a listed building. It was extensively restored in 1994 and 1995, when it became a hotel and conference centre. An office block was added in 2000 to accommodate the staff of the Scouts in the UK. Today, the estate covers more than 100 acres, most of which is a campsite and activity centre.

Inside the White House, among many other artefacts, are nine Scout-related paintings by Ernest Carlos that were created between 1910 and 1914. These pictures were almost as important in promoting the concept of Scouting as *Scouting for Boys*.

The Wood Badge

Since September 1919, Scout Leaders have been awarded the Wood Badge when they complete their training. This iconic symbol of Scouting has become shrouded in myth. But, after extensive research, the story has now been pieced together.

Souvenirs from Africa

The Wood Badge's design was inspired by a necklace that Baden-Powell brought back from Africa. In 1888, during his service with the British Army, B-P visited an abandoned camp where Chief Dinizulu, a local chief, had been based. He recalled what he found:

'In the hut, which had been put up for Dinizulu to live in, I found among other things his necklace of wooden beads. I had in my possession a photograph of him taken a few months beforehand, in which he was shown wearing this necklace round his neck and one shoulder.'

B-P described the chief as 'full of resources, energy and pluck' – characteristics he would later call upon Scouts to develop. He took the necklace as a souvenir of the campaign, and referred to it as Dinizulu's necklace from then on.

Then in 1900, Baden-Powell was the British Army Commander during the Siege of Mafeking, part of the second Boer War in South Africa. While there, he met an elderly African man who wore a leather lace around his neck that his mother had given him for luck. The man then gave this gift to Baden-Powell.

Chief Dinizulu, photographed around the time Baden-Powell found the necklace.

Wanted: Scout Leaders

Following World War One, at least 7,000 Scouts and adult volunteers had been killed during the conflict, but youth membership had grown by more than 46,000. These young Scouts needed leaders, and the leaders needed to be trained. In November 1918, Gilwell Park, on the edge of Epping Forest, was bought, and it soon became a training centre for leaders.

Events for leader training had been held before the war, but the Wood Badge course was the first formal course on offer. In early 1919, East London Commissioner Percy Bantock Nevill arranged a theoretical and administrative course for Scout Leaders. He was in the process of organising a practical training camp when Gilwell Park was purchased. He took advantage of this new facility and held his practical training camp on 18–19 May 1919.

Scout Headquarters wanted to create a training syllabus for leaders to ensure high standards and consistency. A pilot course was scheduled at Gilwell Park from 8–19 September 1919. In August 1919, Baden-Powell wrote to Percy Everett, who was helping to develop the course, asking for his opinion on how leaders who had completed their training should

be rewarded. He suggested that those who complete the course should have a badge to wear, perhaps 'a tassel with ornamented ends to be worn in the hat'.

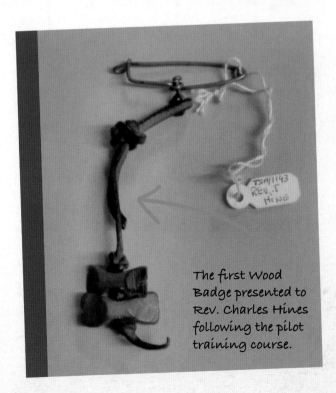

The first Wood Badge presented to Rev. Charles Hines following the pilot training course.

This was still under discussion when the course started. On 15 September 1919 Eileen Nugent, Baden-Powell's secretary, wrote to Percy Everett saying:

'The Chief Scout has suggested to Capt. Gidney the following decoration for Scoutmasters passing the training course, in place of the cords around the hat a bead at the end of the lacing of the hat in three grades:

• Wood

• Bronze

• White metal

He has asked Capt. Gidney to go ahead in getting some beads made (like those of the Chief's which you have) ready for award at the end of the course.'

We can assume that she was referring to the beads from the Chief's necklace that Baden-Powell had collected 40 years previously.

The original beads

The design of the Wood Badge continued to evolve. In 1921, the first description of the Wood Badge in POR (Policy, Organisation and Rules) describes the badge as being worn: 'strung on a leather bootlace round the neck'. It doesn't mention the different levels of the badge, or it being worn around a hat.

Deputy Camp Chiefs could wear a set of four beads. At this time, only two sets of six wood beads were created, and were worn by B-P and Everett. All six beads on both necklaces came from Dinizulu's necklace. In 1949, Everett presented his set to John Thurman, Camp Chief at Gilwell Park, decreeing that they should be passed down to each successor of that role. This continued until 2015, when the set of beads was retired. Both sets of six beads are now held in the Scouts UK heritage collection and the role of Camp

Chief at Gilwell Park is an honorary title held by the Chief Operating Officer.

The beads from the original necklace quickly ran out, and Scout Leaders were asked to return their Wood Badges when they left Scouting so they could be recycled. At some point in the early 1920s, Haydn Dimmock, editor of The Scout magazine, sourced an alternative necklace:

'... it was there, on a [Portobello Road] stall literally crowded with junk and so-called antiques, that I discovered a genuine Zulu necklace similar to that which the Chief Scout had secured from Donizuli (sic) the Zulu Chief, the wooden beads from which historic necklace were used for the original Wood Badges given to Scouts passing the Wood Badge course of training.'

These beads were used for a while to supplement the dwindling supply of 'original' beads, until they, too, ran out!

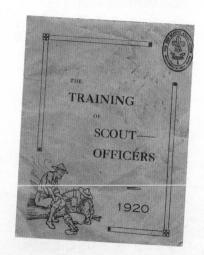

THE TRAINING OF SCOUT OFFICERS

1920

The pilot course

The organisation of the training course was modelled on a Scout Troop structure. Participants were formed into patrols and the roles of Patrol Leader and Assistant were rotated amongst the group. As well as sessions on practical skills, specialist lectures were held on topics from Industrial Welfare to the Education Act and Rover Scouting. The course ended with a visit to the Scout Headquarters on Buckingham Palace Road in London and a lunch meeting with Baden-Powell.

The pilot Wood Badge course participants with Francis Gidney, who took on the role of Scoutmaster, and Baden-Powell.

The Gidney Cabin was later built in 1929 and named after Francis Gidney.

The First Wood Badge

The Rev. Charles Hines attended the pilot course. He later recalled how he received his Wood Badge created by Baden-Powell using one of the beads from Dinizulu's necklace:

'This historic necklace consisted of small hornbeam beads, shaped like miniature, double-edged axe heads, tightly threaded, criss-cross, on a leather thong which was as stiff as a backbone. Taking one of these beads and a replica made from Epping Hornbeam, B-P threaded them on a short leather lace, tied to a brass curtain hook, pinned it on my lapel and announced that he had decided to make it the official award for efficiency in woodcraft and camp management – and to be known as the Dinizulu Woodcraft Badge. He then presented to each of my brother officers one of the original beads together with a small piece of Epping Hornbeam from which to shape a duplicate and assemble their badge.'

Next steps

The pilot Wood Badge course had been a success, but not all future leaders could spare ten days to attend. On 17 October 1919, Baden-Powell wrote to Francis Gidney to discuss what they had learnt from the pilot.

He suggested that the theoretical and administrative training could be completed over the winter months, with the practical residential being carried out over the summer. He also discussed the design for a Wood Badge in a letter to Gidney:

'After passing the theoretical and practical course satisfactorily, the candidate would be entitled to wear one wooden bead on the button hole.

'After passing all three satisfactorily, one bead on the hat string and a Diploma. If he shows special capability and ability for training others as a local Camp or Circle Chief, he could wear the double bead on a hat string.'

In November 1919, the new training structure was announced in the *Headquarters Gazette*.

The Gilwell Oak

The Gilwell Oak has become renowned throughout the world. Baden-Powell used the oak tree as an analogy for the growth and development of Scouting. He referred to the Brownsea Island experimental camp as the acorn from which the oak tree of Scouting grew.

New location

The current Gilwell Oak is the second to bear this name. The previous one was located in Branchet Field, but had to be taken down in the mid 1950s after it became unsafe. The current Gilwell Oak sits on the edge of the training ground, the area in which Scout volunteers stayed to complete the residential aspect of their training. When they returned home, many Scouts set up their own training centres to pass on their learning. The legend of Gilwell spread around the world and the idyllic scene of Scouts taking shelter from the summer sun (or rain) under the branches of this iconic tree became well known.

Tree of the year

In 2017 the Gilwell Oak's story led to it winning the title of the Woodland Trust's UK Tree of the Year. The oak tree continues to be an important symbol in Scouting. The Young Leaders' Badge shows an acorn and leaves and the adult awards include the Silver Acorn. The Silver Acorn is an award presented to adult volunteers in the UK Scouts for distinguished service to Scouting.

Silver Acorn Award

Young Leaders' Award

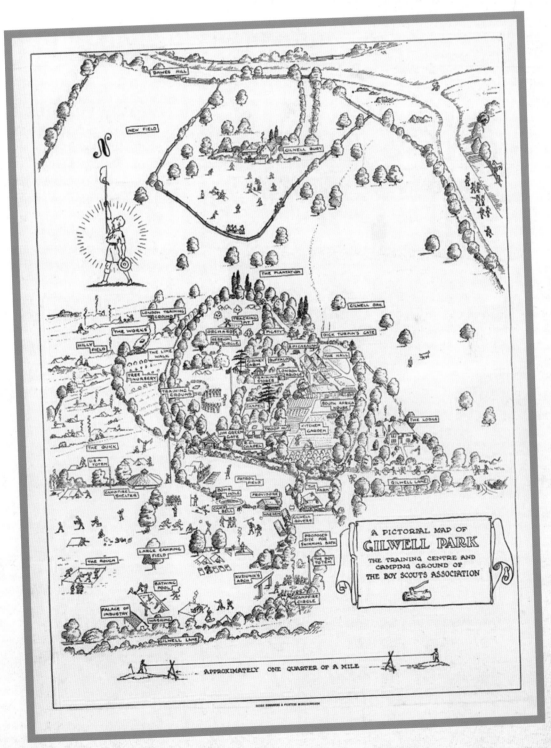

APPROXIMATELY ONE QUARTER OF A MILE

Lasting legacies

Gilwell Park is scattered with memorials to those who have made significant contributions to Scouting. Dorothy Hughes and Betty Melville Smith are two such people.

Dorothy Hughes

Dorothy Hughes was born in the 1890s into an affluent family. She devoted her adult life to working with young people. In the 1920s she moved to the Dockland area of West Ham where she ran several Cub Packs.

Dorothy carried on her work with the section during World War Two while also running an Auxiliary Ambulance Station. She bought a Scout hall for her group and later contributed funds towards the Dorothy Hughes Pack Holiday Centre. This is still used by thousands of young people every year.

When she passed away in 1973 her obituary gave her the epitaph, 'She was born with a silver spoon but used it to feed others.'

An accommodation block in Gilwell Park was named The Dorothy Hughes Pack Holiday Centre in 1970.

In 1958, Dorothy was awarded the Silver Wolf.

Betty Melville Smith

Many groups that have visited Gilwell will have been told to stow their equipment in 'Rikki's Store', but who was Rikki? Rikki was the nickname of Betty Melville Smith. Her association with the Cubs began in 1925 with the 5th Hong Kong (Peak) Pack, which included Cubs of seven nationalities. When she returned to Britain she was based in Birmingham and ran several packs, including one based at an open-air hospital. During World War Two she was involved with a Scout group for evacuees, which she described as 'difficult'.

In 1945, she was awarded the Silver Acorn, appointed the HQ Wolf Cubs Secretary, and in 1958 she received the Silver Wolf. Her service continued through the delivery of Cub Leader training at Gilwell Park until 1969. In 1979, she attended Gilwell Reunion at the age of 93, still relishing the opportunity to immerse herself in the Scouting world.

She died in 1983. Rikki was modest about her achievements and on an HQ form asking about hobbies and achievements, she described herself as 'not brilliant in any way'. Her list of great achievements for Scouting would appear to dispute that!

Betty ran Cub Packs during World War Two.

The first jamboree

In 1920, a huge Scouting event took place at London Olympia. This is now referred to as the first World Scout Jamboree, but it bore little comparison with those that followed. It was an indoor exhibition intended to give the public the opportunity to see what Scouting was all about.

The spirit of brotherhood

Baden-Powell wanted to hold an international event to mark the movement's tenth anniversary in June 1918. Its objective was: 'to make our ideals and methods more widely known abroad; to promote the spirit of brotherhood among the rising generation throughout the world...'. He proposed that items made by Scouts should be on show, and that displays of activities and competitions in Scoutcraft would

feature. Writing in the Headquarters Gazette in July 1920, he said: 'It is to mark the restoration of peace, to render homage to the Scouts who have fallen, and to inaugurate the era of reconstruction and better world relations all round. The occasion would be incomplete if we did not invite our brother Scouts from overseas, not only those who are our close allies but those who remained neutral and even those who were for the time being our enemies, where they exist.'

Planning and preparation

The biggest challenge was one of accommodation. The Scouts taking part in performances would sleep at Olympia, but finding a camp for the rest within reach of the exhibition hall was not easy. More than 15 spots were visited, but there were problems with each of them. The Scouts were then granted permission to use the Old Deer Park in Richmond as a camp for 3,000. The floor of the Olympia great hall was covered with one foot of earth so that Scouts could pitch their tents!

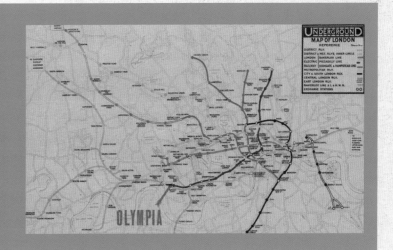

Displays and competitions

The exhibition included objects made by Scouts, such as toys, rugs and walking sticks, as well as working models of steam engines and aeroplanes. One part of the building became a zoo, with a lioness cub from Rhodesia, an alligator from Florida, a baby crocodile from Jamaica, monkeys from South Africa, a baby elephant and a camel, among other smaller animals and birds. Competitions were planned for stamp collections, scrapbooks and bugle playing. Displays of boxing, wrestling, dancing and physical training, as well as dealing with accidents or natural disasters, were also planned. There was an exhibition on woodcraft, which included hike tents, rafts and other outdoor objects.

The Jamboree was officially opened on Friday 31 July. The next day, 15,000 people witnessed the Grand Procession of Nations. By Monday, the weather had changed for the worse. Torrential rain left parts of the campsite at Richmond under water. Olympia, on the other hand, was flooded only with people – 14,000 visited on this day alone.

Missions across the country

One popular feature of the programme was a long-distance dispatch carrying competition. Eight routes were selected for Scouts to carry written messages over long distances by relay. Five of the journeys were known as the 'Giant's routes', which were from Grimsby, York, Exeter, Liverpool and Carmarthen. Three others, the 'Pilgrim's routes', were from Hastings, Norwich and Portsmouth. The idea was that each Scout should travel only a few miles from home, but due to holidays and summer camps, the Scouts who carried the dispatches had to travel for up to 16 kilometres (10 miles). Many of these journeys were undertaken in pouring rain!

Another event was the marathon long-distance ride, in which teams of three Scouts had to travel to Olympia from a start point more than 160 kilometres (100 miles) away, carrying all their food, utensils and sleeping equipment on their bicycles. Their route had to take them at least 48 hours, with two nights of camping.

'Noisy revel'

The word 'jamboree' was already in existence, meaning 'noisy revel, a carousal or spree' in American slang. When later asked why he chose this word to describe a world camp of Scouts, Baden-Powell reflected on this dictionary definition, and said, 'What else could you call it?'

A new brotherhood

The significance of the Jamboree became clear over the course of the event. What had started as a rally had developed into a demonstration of international goodwill. The Scout movement had come into its own and the public recognised it for what it was: a new brotherhood that knew no boundaries of race, creed or colour. The national press gave unprecedented coverage to the Jamboree, which attracted more spectators than the building could cope with. Many had to be turned away.

On the final evening, Baden-Powell was acclaimed as Chief Scout of the World in what must have been an electrifying atmosphere. After a rousing speech, the last post was sounded in memory of the Scouts who had fallen during the war. There was then a two-minute silence before 'Auld Lang Syne' was played, after which Baden-Powell was lifted up shoulder-high and carried across the arena amidst great cheers!

Stalls demonstrated different aspects of the growing Scout family.

The moment at which Baden-Powell was acclaimed as Chief Scout of the World.

The practice of publishing a daily jamboree newspaper – the *Daily Scout* – began at the first World Scout Jamboree.

Friendship between nations

At the end of the first jamboree, a few lessons had been learned. An indoor exhibition limits the activities and prevents a full demonstration of Scouting. As a result, later jamborees were held in outdoor camps. It was noted that the public was mainly attracted by the happiness of the Scouts rather than by spectacular displays. Above all else, a jamboree is a manifestation of friendship between young people from many nations.

Another result of the Jamboree was that the International Conference was established – or the World Scout Conference as it was later to become – which would meet every two years. One of the first achievements of the conference was the publication of Jamboree, a quarterly magazine about world Scouting.

A more unfortunate outcome was that the Jamboree's deficit, estimated at £14,000, left the movement almost bankrupt. What had been a potential goldmine had turned into a financial mess. The number of Scouts also declined the following year (although the number of leaders increased). However, this did not deter Baden-Powell from pressing ahead with plans for even more ambitious events.

A ticket to the 1920 Jamboree.

Baden-Powell inspecting Cubs.

Countries represented at the first World Scout Jamboree:

Australia	Luxembourg
Belgium	Malaya
Ceylon	Malta
Chile	Netherlands
China	New Zealand
Czechoslovakia	Norway
Denmark	Portugal
England	Romania
Estonia	Scotland
France	Serbia
Gibraltar	Siam
Greece	South Africa
India	Spain
Ireland	Sweden
Italy	Switzerland
Jamaica	United States of America
Japan	Wales

Rover Scouts

With Wolf Cubs, younger Scouts had been catered for. The next question was how to keep Scouts involved once they had left school, so the Rover Scouts were created for older teenagers.

In September 1918, at the end of World War One, the *Headquarters Gazette* reported that a new Scout section should cater for 'returning heroes'. The existing scheme for Senior Scouts was unpopular, so the name was changed to Rover Scouts, which hinted at adventure and freedom. In the Chief Scout's view, Rovers Scouts were: 'a brotherhood of the Open Air and Service. They are hikers on the Open Road and Campers of the Wood.' Their uniform was identical to that of a Scout but with their own badges, red garter tabs, epaulettes, and a thumb-stick in place of the Scout stave. By November 1919 the Rover Scout section was firmly established. Baden-Powell wrote:

'The Rover stage is the third progressive step in the education of the Boy Scout.

But you can't hold a lad without giving him some definite objectives and activities.

So we offer Service:

1. Service to self, career, health
2. Service to the Scout movement
3. Service to the community.'

According to the Chief Scout, service was the means by which a Rover Scout fulfilled his promise of duty to God. The concept of 'Brotherhood and Service' became the Rover Scouts' motto. Rover Patrols became known as Crews, and each Crew's leader was a Rover Mate. Finally, a gathering of Rovers from different places was called a Moot.

Mythical symbolism

Just as the Wolf Cub section was based around Kipling's Mowgli and *The Jungle Book*, the legends of King Arthur and his valiant Knights of the Round Table became the inspiration for the Rovers. It proved rich in symbolism, with terms such as Squire, Vigils and Quest. Scout shops began to sell bronze replicas of a statue that had been sculpted by Baden-Powell himself: that of a kneeling knight offering up his sword as an act of total self-dedication.

Rovering to Success

Baden-Powell wrote a book for the Rover Scouts called *Rovering to Success* (1922), which became another bestseller. It offered advice on a range of topics, and B-P received letters from parents asking for solutions to problems they were having with their teenagers. The magazine *Rover World* was also published at this time.

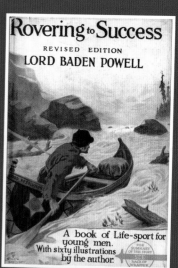

A Rover's quest

After an elaborate initiation ceremony, involving a knight mentor and a St George's Cross flag, the Rover Scout could embark on his Quest, like King Arthur's knights. There were quests for: truth, world Scouting, Rover errantry, supporting younger siblings, beauty, kindness to animals, conscience, happiness, personal efficiency and the spiritual.

The idea of quests inspired Rover Scouts to take up community projects. Some Crews specialised in First Aid or voluntary work in local hospitals. Rovers in Leyton, east London, ran an early Citizens' Advice Bureau, while others looked after young people on probation.

Rover Scouting had few rules to start with, but without clear ground rules, this arm of Scouting had little to unify it. After a conference held at Scout Headquarters in October 1921, the minimum age for Rovers was set at 17. The section's objective was to retain older Scouts with a view to them becoming leaders in the future. Baden-Powell wrote succinctly in 1928: 'Rover Scouting is a preparation for life, and also a pursuit for life.'

Rover Scouts at the Monzie Moot of 1939.

The Rover Moot

Rovers needed their own version of the jamboree, so the World Scout Moot – an Anglo-Saxon word meaning 'gathering' – was created. The first was held in 1931 at the International Scout Chalet at Kandersteg in Switzerland. It was attended by Rover Scouts from 22 countries. At the second Moot, held in 1935, B-P expressed his hope that the Moots would generate enough goodwill to avoid future conflict amongst nations.

This hope was shattered a few years later when World War Two brought strain and challenges to Scouting. Rover Scouts were among the first to be called up to fight. Consequently, they suffered great losses. Many Crews were suspended during the war and some never reopened. In Britain, the number of Rovers slumped from a pre-war high of 38,000 members to just 7,291 in 1945.

A new beginning

In the 1950s, the age limit for Rovers was revised to 17½ to 24 years and a new scheme was introduced. However, the new ideas were not warmly welcomed and in 1967 the Rover Scout section was disbanded in the UK. It was replaced by Venture Scouts, for those aged between 16 and 21. This was replaced in 2002 by Explorer Scouts, for 14 to 18 year olds, and the Scout Network, for 18 to 25 year olds. Rover Scouting continues to flourish in many countries to this day, giving valuable service to Scouting and the wider community.

Rover Scout Moots

1st	Kandersteg, Switzerland	1931
2nd	Ingarö, Sweden	1935
3rd	Monzie, Scotland	1939
4th	Skjak, Norway	1949
5th	Kandersteg, Switzerland	1953
6th	Sutton Coldfield, England	1957
7th	Melbourne, Australia	1961
8th	Melbourne, Australia	1990–91
9th	Kandetsteg, Switzerland	1992
10th	Ransäter, Sweden	1996
11th	Mexico City, Mexico	2000
12th	Taiwan	2004
13th	Mozambique (cancelled)	2008
14th	Kenya	2010
15th	Canada	2013
16th	Iceland	2017
17th	Ireland	2021

The Scouts come of age

The Scout movement reached its 21st birthday – and 'came of age' – in 1929. Since it began, the movement had grown from small beginnings on Brownsea Island into a worldwide organisation with around two million members.

At this time, the publication of Scouting for Boys in 1908, rather than the Brownsea Island camp, was seen as the launch of Scouting. A big anniversary required a special celebration, so the third World Scout Jamboree was held in the country where it began: the UK.

Arrowe Park

A venue was quickly chosen when the Mayor of Birkenhead offered the use of Arrowe Park, near Liverpool. It was a 450-acre site with woodlands, a hall for meetings and receptions, good transport facilities and a nearby port. The name 'Arrowe Park' gave Baden-Powell the idea for the Jamboree's symbol: a Golden Arrow.

Making the best of it

The Duke of Connaught, the President of the UK Scouts, opened the Jamboree on 31 July 1929, and B-P blasted on the kudu horn that had been used on Brownsea Island. Heavy rain and gales soon made the site muddy. The French area suffered the worst damage, but a model Eiffel Tower made from Scout staffs rose above the bad weather. The rain and mud strengthened, rather than dampened, the Scout spirit!

In his speech, B-P joked that whenever he visited a Jamboree, it rained. 'I don't like you all to feel too happy so I turned on the rain. You see, anyone can be a Scout on a fine day, but the thing is to make the best of conditions on a bad day.'

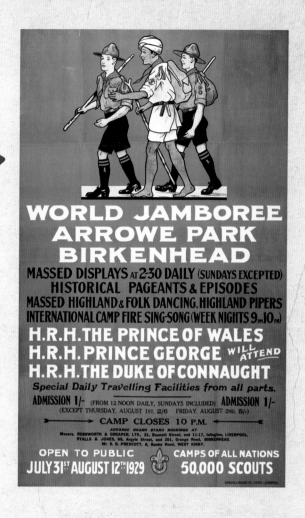

'All the world in miniature'

More than 65 countries, 30,000 Scouts and 320,000 visitors took part. The Scouts marched with their flags, showing the diversity of the youth of the world. A journalist wrote:

'I saw the glory and splendour of the world's boyhood in that English park – all the world in miniature – and tried to peer into the unknown future toward which they go, so keen… so gallant… without fear. [...] A grey, lean old man, with a tanned, leathery face and twinkling eyes under his Scout's hat, watched this living pageant of an idea that had come into his head. [...] Tonight, round the campfires, they will sing their national songs and dance their old folk dances. It is a fairy-tale come true.'

The UK leaders of the world faiths gathered to worship. Cardinal Bourne of Westminster said that at that moment in time only Scouting could bring together leaders of different religious faiths around one table.

Lord Baden-Powell was joined by the
Prince of Wales at the 1929 Jamboree.

News from the King

The Prince of Wales (later to become King Edward VIII) attended in his capacity as Chief Scout of Wales. He arrived on 1 August and stayed for several days. In a speech, he brought a message from his father, King George V. He announced that to mark this great event in Scouting's history, Baden-Powell was being made a Baron. The news was received with enthusiastic cheers. Baden-Powell wanted to refuse the honour but was persuaded to accept it as recognition of the movement's work as well as his own. He consulted with the World Scout Committee about his new title and chose 'Lord Baden-Powell of Gilwell'. This signified how much Gilwell Park meant to him – and to the movement – as the home of Scouting, where his vision was being lived out each day.

Other ceremonies and displays were held each afternoon, including a Wolf Cub rally, and the French enacted the life of St Joan of Arc while the Belgians staged the story of St George and the dragon.

B-P blasted the kudu horn to open
the 1929 Jamboree.

The badge for the 1929 Jamboree.

A pair of braces

Scouts were invited to contribute to a present for Baden-Powell. Olave had asked him whether there was anything he needed, to which he replied 'a pair of braces' to hold up his trousers. On 10 August, Baden-Powell was given his present. He received a Rolls-Royce car, which was nicknamed 'Jam Roll' as a play on the names 'Jamboree' and 'Rolls-Royce', a caravan named 'Eccles' after the caravan's manufacturers, a cheque for £2,800 and an oil painting of Baden-Powell by David Jaggar. He later received the new pair of braces he had desired, much to his delight, from the Irish Scouts.

Brothers in every country

At the close of the Jamboree, Scouts formed lines like wheel spokes with Baden-Powell at the centre, looking like the hub of a great wheel. Their founder said, 'Here is buried the hatchet of war, of enmity, of bad feeling, which I now bury in Arrowe,' and with that, he buried an axe. Large, wooden, golden arrows were then handed down the lines to the heads of the international contingents. He added:

'From all corners of the world you come to the call of brotherhood and to Arrowe. Now I send you forth to your homeland, bearing the sign of peace and goodwill and fellowship to all your fellow men. From now on the symbol of peace and goodwill is the golden arrow. Carry that arrow on and on, so that all may know of the brotherhood of men.

'I want you to go back from here to your countries [...] with a new idea in your mind of having brothers in every country. You have seen them and you know them now, personally [...] Go forth from here as ambassadors of good will and friendship.'

The Gang Show

In 1929, the Rover Scouts of Holborn in London staged a one-night show called 'Good Turns', written by an anonymous 'Holborn Scout'. Similar productions followed, and three years later, the shows had a considerable reputation. A West End production was planned. The show went on.

Within an hour of the proposal, a programme had been compiled, and within the next few days, a cast of 120 people had been recruited. The Holborn Rover Scouts carried the organisational burden, assisted by the 4th Harrow Rovers. At the first rehearsal, they were all told that everyone took part on an equal basis, and that anyone with lines or a song was just fortunate. This remains the tradition today.

The Gang's All Here

One night during rehearsals, the cast came together after a break and the producer asked, 'Are they all back?' to which a piping voice answered, 'Aye, aye, Skip, the gang's all 'ere'. The young, cockney Scout had accidentally given the West End show its title: *The Gang's All Here*.

The Scala theatre in London was booked for three performances of *The Gang's All Here*. Some thought that selling nearly 5,000 tickets for a Scout show was impossible. But they went ahead, despite many problems and several unsold tickets. The three performances were momentous evenings. Songs such as 'Steer for the Open Sea' and 'There'll Come a Time Some Day' were highlights, and the show ended to cheers and curtain calls.

The Gang Comes Back

Much to their surprise, the first show had made a profit of £150, and there was support for a second show the following year. The Gang Comes Back was planned for 1933, and the same theatre booked six evening performances and a matinée. Every seat was sold within a few weeks of the box office opening! The drama critics of the national newspapers took notice and theatre professionals were encouraged to see it. They left asking for seats for the following night.

By the time the production finished, 'Gang Shows' were established as a firm part of the Scouting landscape. Scouts outside London began to stage their own Gang Shows using material from the London show with local casts. For the next London show in 1934, every seat was sold before the opening performance.

The show must go on

Baden-Powell's enthusiasm for the Gang Show ensured that it would continue. He wrote: 'You have made a big success – may we have more', and later, 'I am not merely thinking of the acting, good though it was, but of the splendid teamwork of the whole lot. It must go on and on.'

In 1935, the identity of the 'Holborn Rover' became known: Ralph Reader, West End producer and active Scout. He did not willingly own up to his role and the revelation nearly destroyed his professional career, as many of his theatre colleagues struggled to accept someone who worked with amateurs.

At the Royal Albert Hall

In 1936, Reader staged the musical pageant play Boy Scout at the Royal Albert Hall. It told the story of a boy joining a Scout Troop and his life with the Scouts, ending with a jamboree. With a cast of 1,200, a choir of 250, catchy music and colourful costumes and scenery, it was a spectacle that played to packed houses for three performances. It was even more successful the following year.

There were more than 150 productions at the Royal Albert Hall, including the British Legion Festival of Remembrance. For millions of Scouts, Ralph Reader would always be 'Mr Gang Show', to whom the movement owes an enormous debt.

Saying goodbye

In July 1937, Baden-Powell was warmly welcomed at the World Scout Jamboree held in the Netherlands. The Founder was now aged 80 and his thoughts were turning at last to retirement, and relinquishing responsibility for his beloved movement.

'God bless you all'

'The time has come', he said in his closing speech, 'for me to say goodbye. You know that many of us will never meet again in this world. I am in my eighty-first year and am nearing the end of my life. Most of you are at the beginning, and I want your lives to be happy and successful. You can make them so by doing your best to carry out the Scout Law all your days, whatever your station and wherever you are.'

He bade the Scouts a moving farewell: 'Now goodbye. God bless you all!' His voice faltered, but after a pause, he swung his Scout hat over his head, repeating loudly and strong: 'God bless you all!'

He was right – that was the last time he appeared on the world stage.

A cottage in Kenya

To mark the Baden-Powells' silver wedding anniversary in October 1937, a dinner party for over 300 Scouters and Guiders was held in London. The couple received a collection of silver plates plus a cheque for £2,600. Shortly afterwards, while on holiday in Kenya, a medical check-up on B-P showed that he had a tired heart.

On hearing about his punishing schedule for the months ahead, his doctor prescribed complete rest for a year. The Baden-Powells then decided to use the silver wedding money to build a small cottage in the grounds of the Outspan Hotel, in the shadow of Mount Kenya. They named this cottage 'Paxtu'. It was their second home to be called Pax, and 'Paxtu' means complete peace in Swahili.

Waving goodbye to England

Baden-Powell returned to England for the last time in 1938 to tie up his affairs. He knew the Scout movement was in good hands under Lord Somers. When the ship docked, he came to the deck rail to wave at the thousands of Scouts and Guides who had come to see their Chief.

He and Olave left their home, Pax Hill, and England together for the last time in October 1938 to begin a new life. They settled into their new home well, and Baden-Powell resumed his love of painting, producing some striking scenes of African wildlife.

One of B-P's sketches of life in Kenya.

War and Peace

In 1939, Baden-Powell had been nominated for the Nobel Peace Prize in recognition of his achievements promoting world peace through the Scout movement, and through Jamborees in particular. Unfortunately, the prize was not awarded that year, due to the outbreak of World War Two.

When war broke out, Baden-Powell wrote to Lord Somers offering to return home if he could help. Somers gently declined the offer and assured him that the Scout movement would live up to its every expectation.

World War Two and beyond

1939–1966

War service

With the outbreak of World War
Two, the worldwide Scout movement
was ready to play its part. A National
Service Badge had been introduced
in Britain. During the course of World
War Two, more than 60,000 Scouts
in Britain over the age of 14 were
awarded this badge.

The movement organised and took part in hundreds of activities. Scouts worked as Air Raid Precaution messengers, First Aid orderlies and telephonists, instructors to the Home Guard and assistants in rest centres. Scouts made thousands of camouflage nets and turned coal dust into briquettes for the Ministry of Fuel and Power.

Scouts helped to construct air raid shelters.

1st MOLESCROFT SCOUTS FIRE SERVICE.

During the air raids

It was during the air raids that many Scouts provided outstanding service. Scouts over the age of 14 could be used as indoor messengers or for duties defending their country, as long as they went to shelters during air raids.

In Glasgow, for example, the under-16s formed 'after-the-raid-squads' who set to work the moment that the 'all clear' sounded. They rescued victims buried under the debris of bombed houses, salvaged furniture, looked after helpless children and assisted at Rest Centres and Canteens.

Scouts built more than 40,000 Morrison shelters, manufactured homemade torch batteries, and assembled, distributed, repaired and disinfected gas masks. They also provided film shows and other entertainment in air raid shelters. Many householders who had been indifferent to Scouting began to understand the movement and appreciate the Scouts' training.

During the great blitz on London, fire brigades were summoned from all surrounding areas. Scouts met the fire engines on the outskirts of the city and guided them to where they were needed via the quickest route.

Many lives were saved by Scouts, but some lost their own lives while on air raid duty. More than 80 Scouts were given an award for their gallantry.

Evacuees

In 1939 the threat of air raids and gas attacks on British cities led to over one million children being sent to the countryside for safety. Many Packs and Troops moved with the children as they were evacuated out of cities. Scouts also helped with the evacuation process by helping to organise groups of children, carry luggage and offer comfort.

Scouts helped tired children to carry their luggage as they were evacuated from cities.

Once children settled into their new homes, Scouting gave them a sense of familiarity.

Helpers and messengers

Scout messengers often cycled amongst falling shell fragments carrying information from fire engines to control points. Scouts worked in hospitals alongside the medical staff, equipped and manned ambulance tents and assisted with X-rays. During the evacuations, they acted as escorts and guides, erected temporary toilets, distributed clothing, packed and distributed rations and cleaned and repaired houses that were used as temporary accommodation. During the daytime, they painted street corners and kerbs white and blacked-out private and public buildings.

Scout premises and equipment were used to help refugees. Scouts also assisted with milk rounds. Scouts also treated injured animals and converted their trek carts to animal ambulances.

No job was too small for the Scouts during wartime.

SCOUT SERVICE
★ LET US HELP YOU

For the duration of the War the Scouts and Cubs of Kenton are organised to serve the Community.

ALL SERVICE ENTIRELY FREE
NO REASONABLE TASK DECLINED

A Messenger? An escort after dark? Someone to run an errand?

Do You Want — A "Handyman" to do a job which someone in your home could have done if the war hadn't intervened?

Or even a Bathchair attendant?

THEN CALL, WRITE OR PHONE:

KENTON SCOUT SERVICE BUREAU,
Open daily 9 a.m. to 8 p.m.
7a, Radstock Avenue, Kenton.
Phone: WORdsworth 2664.

The Bureau is an Authorised Receiving Depot for

WASTE PAPER

the collection of which has been entrusted to the Boy Scout Movement by the Ministry of Supply. Please phone or write for a Collector to call.

THE HILL PRESS, 6a STATION ROAD, WEALDSTONE.

Scouts and Guides piled up sandbags to protect vulnerable houses.

Scouts carried messages to telephone and telegram operators.

Forbidden Scouts

The only area of the UK to be occupied by the Nazis was the Channel Islands. The invaders had banned Scouting, but at least one troop continued to meet under the nose of the occupying power. In *The Scout* on 21 June 1945, Patrol Leader Vernon Carey of the 11th Jersey Scout Troop wrote about the experience:

'In July 1940 we were occupied by the Germans and, of course, all Scouts were forbidden. At that time I was in the Wolf Cubs. But our Assistant Scoutmaster, Mr. Guy, carried on for about a year and a half with four Scouts, keeping very secret all the time, for we did not know what the Germans were going to do with us...

'We met at one of the Patrol Leader's houses and made a little hut outside our headquarters. We were there for about a year and a half, when one day the

Gestapo raided the house. Luckily, we were not there at the time, but they found a wireless, ammunition and photographs, all forbidden by the Germans.

'On VE Day we had a hurried meeting, dragging out old uniforms, and went into town, a very happy and jubilant band.'

Carrying on

While all this was going on, Scout Troops continued to meet in the absence of thousands of leaders on war service, camping with camouflaged tents and extinguishing their fires after dark. By September 1941, the numbers of warranted Leaders had dropped by more than half, from 44,000 to 21,000. This meant Patrol Leaders were given more responsibility and many Troops were run entirely under boy leadership.

Wartime visit to Canada

In 1942, the Canadian Boy Scouts Association invited four King's Scouts from the UK to tour Canada, telling stories of the part Scouts had played in Britain's civil defence. Stanley Newton from London, John Bethel from Birkenhead, Hugh Bright from Glasgow and Roy Davis from Southampton were selected, all of whom had helped out during the heavy air raids. The tour lasted for 14 weeks, during which time the party covered 13,000 miles and visited 135 cities and towns. They broadcast on 14 occasions, addressed 100 Scout rallies, were guest speakers at 17 service club meetings, spoke at 28 schools, gave talks at six churches and addressed 27 gatherings of Civil Defence personnel. On their return to Britain, the party divided into pairs and, with the support of the Ministry of Information, toured the country telling stories of their experience in North America.

After Baden-Powell

On 8 January 1941, Baden-Powell died at the age of 83. A funeral was held in Kenya, and a memorial service was held at Westminster Abbey. He had already chosen his successor.

Olave's vigil

Baden-Powell's health slowly deteriorated and he developed a form of skin cancer. He was treated with radium that was shipped out to Kenya at the express orders of the British government. He grew slowly weaker, but rallied occasionally, with Olave constantly at his bedside, day and night, and with visits from children and grandchildren.

Olave wrote in her diary on 8 January 1941, 'At 2.30am Sister woke me, saying "he is going". I went to his room and just sat on his bed. He was quite unconscious and still, breathing slowly... At 5am I thought he would still see the day through and went back to bed to get warm. I kissed his dear forehead and Sister Ray stayed by him. And as I lay listening she suddenly came at 5.45 – "He is gone". He looked so sweet and perfect in death as he was in life – utterly, utterly noble and good and dear and wonderful, great and faultless.'

The founder's grave in Nyeri, Kenya, shows the tracking symbol for 'gone home', used on many Scout memorials.

Resting place

Baden-Powell was offered a grave in the central aisle of the nave of Westminster Abbey, between that of the Unknown Warrior and David Livingstone, but Olave considered the Abbey too dull and gloomy. Instead, she wanted him laid to rest among 'the quiet of Gilwell with birdsong and wind in the trees'. He was in fact buried in Nyeri, Kenya, where she could be near him.

Final messages

Baden-Powell left behind several written messages to Scouts, Guides and to the public. He wrote some of these in the 1920s and sealed them until his death. He also left a letter for Olave, expressing his love, and hope that her courage will ease her loss. His final letter, written just a few days before his death, was to King George V's private secretary, asking him to tell the King of his loyalty and thanks.

Dear Scouts,

If you have ever seen the play, Peter Pan, you will remember how the pirate chief was always making his dying speech, because he was afraid that possibly, when the time came for him to die, he might not have time to get it off his chest.

It is much the same with me; and so, although I am not at this moment dying, I shall be doing so one of these days, and I want to send you a parting word of goodbye. Remember, it is the last time you will ever hear from me, so think it over. I have had a most happy life, and I want each and every one of you to have as happy a life too. I believe that God put us in this jolly world to be happy and enjoy life. Happiness does not come from being rich, nor merely from being successful in your career, nor by self-indulgence.

One step towards happiness is to make yourself healthy and strong while you are a boy, so that you can be useful, and so can enjoy life when you are a man. Nature study will show you how full of beautiful and wonderful things God has made the world for you to enjoy. Be contented with what you have got, and make the best of it; look on the bright side of things instead of the gloomy one. But the real way to get happiness is by giving out happiness to other people. Try and leave this world a little better that you found it, and when your turn comes to die you can die happy in feeling that at any rate you have not wasted your time but have done your best.

'Be Prepared' in this way, to live happy and to die happy; stick to your Scout Promise always – even after you have ceased to be a boy – and God help you to do it.

Your friend,
Baden-Powell

Baden-Powell's successor

Shortly after his death, on 29 January, the Council of the Association appointed Lord Somers, the man that Baden-Powell himself had chosen to carry on the work he started, as Chief Scout.

Somers wasted no time in making his mark. A few months later, he wrote in *The Scouter*: 'We propose to build a Memorial House to commemorate our Founder. This will be a great centre in London, dedicated to the B-P way of life; a house where Scouts from all parts of the world will be welcome and feel at home; a common meeting ground where the Fourth Scout Law can be seen in practice... We all owe so much happiness and our ability to be useful to our Founder that we shall do all we can to build a worthy memorial to him. I should like to stress, however, that we are not out for something to look at, but something for Scouts to use.' A fund was opened on St George's Day, 1942.

Next, Lord Somers commissioned a review of Scouting and consulted on what young people and adults wanted to take part in after the war.

WE SHALL BUILD A HOUSE TO HIS MEMORY

Olave continues

Baden-Powell's funeral had been planned in secret. It was held the following day in St Peter's Churchyard, Nyeri, with full military honours. Olave did not attend – she had difficulty coping with death ever since her father and sister had committed suicide. Instead, she went away for the day.

She soon threw herself back into her role as World Chief Guide. Olave accepted a 'grace and favour' apartment at Hampton Court Palace, a gift from a grateful King, where she lived for the rest of her life. When Olave died in 1977, her ashes were flown to Kenya and buried with Baden-Powell's grave, reuniting them at last.

Churchill's message to Scouting

The wartime Prime Minister, Winston Churchill, wrote a message to the Scouts, which was read out during a conference on future Scouting in Britain. It said:

I first met B-P many years before the birth of the Scout movement. He was a man of character, vision and enthusiasm and he passed these qualities on to the movement which has played and is playing an important part in moulding the character of our race. Sturdiness, neighbourliness, practical competence, love of country and, above all, in these times, indomitable resolve, daring and enterprise in the face of the enemy, these are the hallmarks of a Scout. You have many practical difficulties under war-time conditions in carrying on your work but with persistence and ingenuity these can be surmounted in Scout fashion and I have no doubt that in your hands the movement will carry on its task with the steadfast will and high courage with which it was founded. 'Be Prepared' to stand up faithfully for Right and Truth however the winds may blow.

Message from the second Chief Scout

This was later followed by a message from Somers:

The spirit of service is the spirit of the true Scout whatever his age or rank. The spirit of the good turn, ever present in peace time, has matured to devoted self-sacrifice in war. In writing to me recently the Prime Minister, Mr. Winston Churchill, said: 'The record of the work of the Boy Scouts during the war on the Home Front is a very fine one.' I think, therefore, the world should be told of some of the acts of heroism and devotion to duty of our Scouts.

Lord Somers, Chief Scout

Relief Service Team being briefed before going overseas.

Helping other people

The Scout have a long history of helping others, from supporting refugees during the World Wars, to raising money for various causes with 'Bob-a-Job' week.

World War Two

During World War Two, the Scouts worked hard to support refugees arriving in the UK. Various organisations, such as the Red Cross, set up relief teams during World War Two. The relief teams were sent to assist refugees and displaced people in areas of conflict. The Scouts established The Scout International Relief Service (SIRS) in 1942, as they were well placed to help with their experience of setting up and organising large camps, teamwork and First Aid.

I want to thank you for helping to give friendly shelter and assistance to our distressed refugee brothers

Baden-Powell

Baden-Powell designed this emotive thank you card for the Scouts, which shows refugees being attacked as they flee a war zone, with Hitler's face shown on the front of a plane.

Bob-a-Job

Scout Leaders registered their interest at volunteering overseas with SIRS, but there still remained the question as to how their work would be funded. Editor of *The Scout*, F. Haydn Dimmock, proposed that Cubs, Scouts and Rovers carry out a 'job' for one day on 20 May 1944, such as cleaning windows, cutting grass, sweeping pathways. For each job they did, they should earn a shilling, known back then as a 'bob'. This campaign became known as 'Bob-a-Job' day and it raised over £32,000 in one weekend to fund SIRS work.

Scoutmaster Geoffrey Crane of Norwich and John Page of Bexhill preparing to go overseas with the Scout International Relief Service.

Built on the success of the Bob-a-Job day in 1944, the first Bob-a-Job weekend was held in 1949. Jobs would vary from cleaning cars, lawn mowers and shoes, to polishing tortoises. Over the years, the phrase 'Bob-a-Job' has become associated with Scouts, showing their eagerness to help others.

Air Scouting takes off

While World War Two was still being fought, the Committee of the Council introduced an Air Scout branch of the movement, on 31 January 1941. This provided an opportunity for boys with a passion for the aeronautical to explore their interests.

High-flying origins

This was not the Scouts' first opportunity to take to the air. The year 1908 had seen Britain's first powered flight. The innovation of flight developed rapidly, and the Airman's Badge was launched in 1911. This required Scouts to make a working model of an aeroplane or airship, fly it for 25 yards, and have a theoretical knowledge of aeroplanes, airships and their engines, as well as hot air balloons.

At the outbreak of World War One, Britain had very few qualified pilots or engineers. In 1917, a scheme was developed for Scouts to learn the basics of aeronautical engineering to supply the Royal Flying Corps (later the RAF) and Royal Naval Air Service with skilled support.

Era of innovation

During the 1920s, many high-profile flights pushed the boundaries of technology and human endurance. These excited public interest and Scouts were no exception. Unofficial Air Scout patrols met to explore the new advancements by making and flying models. In 1927, it was suggested that an Air Scout branch should be developed, following the same model as the Sea Scouts, but the request was denied.

Scout air activities became increasingly popular in the 1930s. Troops with access to air fields and gliding clubs were encouraged to try out air activities and an 'Air Patrols' leaflet was published. By 1941, World War Two provided the incentive for an Air Scouts branch. The country was lacking in people with this technical knowledge, and the Air Scouts provided training for those too young to join the Air Training Corps. During the war, high-profile events and camps were held to promote Air Scouting. These attracted support from celebrities such as the actor Lawrence Olivier (a lieutenant in the Fleet Air Arm). This link with the Armed Forces continued after the war, and from 1950, Air Scout groups could apply to the RAF.

75 years later

The year 2016 marked the 75th birthday of the Air Scouts, and today there are 65 Air Scout groups in the UK carrying on the Scouts' long tradition of aeronautical adventures.

Reconstruction and peace

Throughout the 20th century, whenever a dictatorship seized power – left wing, right wing, fascist, Nazi or communist – one of its first acts was to ban Scouting and Guiding. But the movements continued in whatever form they could.

In many countries where Scouting was abolished, the ruling power introduced their own organisation, as the indoctrination of young people was seen as key to a dictator's survival. Baden-Powell's youth movements encouraged young people to think for themselves, so were seen as a threat. When Poland was invaded in 1939, Scouting was banned by the Germans and it was soon suppressed in other occupied countries. It became a familiar pattern.

By September 1941, 14 Scout countries were under Nazi occupation and four others allied to the Axis powers. In these countries Scouting had to go underground to survive.

Underground Scouting

Some Scouts chose to leave their homes following Nazi occupation. They made the dangerous journey to neutral countries such as Spain. This logbook was created by Scouts who were placed in Camp Miranda, an internment camp in northern Spain. It contains stories written by Polish, Danish, French and Belgium Scouts. Some of them tell of their escape from Nazi oppression and others wrote about their time in the Scouts.

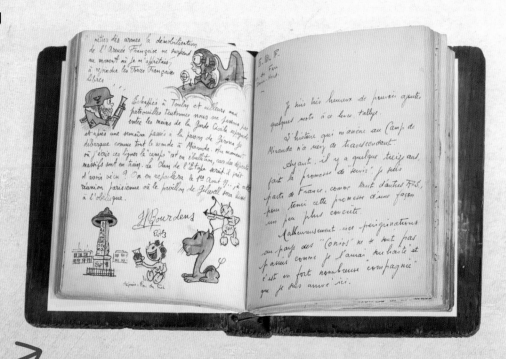

Prisoners of war

Scouting survived in some extraordinary places, including under the noses of the guards in prisoner of war (POW) camps in both Germany and the Far East. In the Japanese civilian POW camps in Singapore, Cub Packs and Scout Troops were set up to give children a sense of structure and purpose. The programme was delivered using the scant resources available and the ingenuity of pre-war leaders. In both German and Japanese POW camps, men from the allied armed forces set up Rover Scout Crews, spending meetings learning from each other and even completing leader training courses. Activities had to be conducted in complete secrecy, as organised meetings were banned.

The men made their own pieces of uniform, such as this wristband from pieces of stolen canvas and scrap metal.

The Changi Rover Crew Log Book. In this, Scouts recorded their activities and observations on life in a POW camp.

Liberation

A country did not have to be completely liberated before Scouting restarted. In Italy, the movement had been abolished by Mussolini in 1927. As the liberating armies moved up from the south, Scout Troops formed behind them. Many of the members wore the uniforms their fathers had worn before the fascist regime. Shortly after the fall of Mussolini, and before any armistice was signed, the new government had authorised the official re-establishment of the movement. A similar pattern was repeated elsewhere.

In August 1944, a scheme was launched in Scotland that enabled Scout groups in one country to be put in contact with a troop in another. This strengthened world Scouting ties through correspondence, exchange visits and camping in other countries, and many international friendships were formed.

The Jamboree of Peace

Another casualty of the war had been the World Scout Jamboree, originally scheduled for France in 1941. Two years after the hostilities ceased, it was at last possible for the 'Jamboree of Peace' to be held – despite immense difficulties. France had been occupied, so supplies of almost everything were limited. The Founder had died and the strength of post-war Scouting was unknown. Staging this Jamboree was therefore a huge challenge. The chosen site was at Moisson, 40 miles northwest of Paris near the river Seine. It was divided into 15 sub-camps named after French provinces. This site became known for its dust and hot weather. It was ten years since the previous Jamboree, so a generation of Scouts had grown up without experiencing such an event.

The organisers need not have worried. Some 25,000 Scouts attended from 70 countries, reflecting a changed world. Many well-known countries were missing, however. For the 200 Scouts from Hungary and 500 from Czechoslovakia, this would be the last time their countries would take part in a jamboree for many years.

But there were signs of hope. There were 200 Scouts, mostly from Baltic countries, who continued their Scouting in 'displaced persons' camps in Austria and Germany. For some, they had lost families and homes and the struggle of adapting to a new life in a new country lay ahead. The participants in this sub-camp made the most of the resources available. For the first few days their cooking pots were made from old biscuit tins.

The jamboree soon took on its usual form, with shows, campfires and shared meals. The decoration of the site, with its towers, stages and gateways, was on a more grandiose scale than anticipated, thanks to the Scouters and Rover Scouts who had laboured during their weekends for many months.

A new dawn for Scouting – and the world

At the closing ceremony after the final speeches, the Chief Scouts from different countries assembled on the arena stage and linked hands to sing 'Auld Lang Syne'. Gradually, everyone else followed. Thousands of people formed a human carrick bend knot, the camp's logo and the sign of the friendship that should exist between all free people.

Proof of this peace came from India and Pakistan, which had been torn apart by civil war between Hindus and Muslims and had become separate countries. A contingent made up of Scouts from both new countries camped together at Moisson, without any violence. The flags of the new countries were broken on flagpoles on either side of the Scout flag, and everyone celebrated the newfound independence of their respective countries. It truly was a Jamboree of Peace.

Golden Jubilee

For Scouts everywhere, 1957 was a special year, marking the centenary of Baden-Powell's birth and 50 years since the Brownsea Island camp.

Thanksgiving service

A National Service of Thanksgiving was held in Westminster Abbey, London. It was a star-studded occasion attended by members of the British royal family, government ministers and the Baden-Powell family. The Archbishop of Canterbury spoke of how the Scout Law was 'wrapped up in doing things, doing interesting things, doing them with others and for others in a spirit of adventure and honour, each bearing his own responsibility and each bearing a bit of everyone else's load… enjoying life by keen living and finding friendship by helping to create it and learning responsibility by sharing it.'

Remembering B-P

Before the service, wreaths were placed on Baden-Powell's memorial stone in the Abbey. On the same day in Nyeri, Kenya, 3,600 Scouts and Guides gathered at Baden-Powell's grave to pay their respects. The jubilee year began with celebrations in every town and country where Scouting existed. Ghana and Malaya both invited Scouts from Britain to be their guests for a few weeks during the summer, two instances of many such gestures of international friendship.

In London, Ralph Reader's play Great Oaks was revived to great acclaim. It followed the story of a young man who joins as a Scout and carries on with his Troop, against changing circumstances, for 50 years. In Glasgow, Scottish Scouts mounted a magnificent exhibition in Kelvin Hall, where the magic of the book Scouting for Boys was brought to life.

Stamps, films and steam engines

But there was more. Commemorative stamps were issued, special issues of magazines and books were published, a film was released about Baden-Powell's life and a railway steam engine was named after the British Chief Scout, Lord Rowallan. And through it all, the main purpose of Scouting – the training of young people in Scouting skills – continued.

World Scout Jamboree-Indaba-Moot

The main celebration was, of course, the ninth World Scout Jamboree, the second World Indaba (or leaders' meeting) and the sixth World Moot, all held together in Sutton Coldfield, a 2,400-acre park of wood and moorland on the outskirts of Birmingham, UK. Heather-clad, with seven lakes and nine entry gates, it was the ideal setting for hosting a canvas town housing 35,000 people from 90 countries, complete with shops, banks, a hospital, a theatre, and police and fire stations. On the designated Cub Day, 30,000 Cubs arrived by train and bus. It was opened on 1 August by the Duke of Gloucester, the President of the UK Scout Association, and closed by the World Chief Guide twelve days later.

An international celebration

The camp followed the now well-established pattern of jamborees – making friends, swapping badges, the national arena displays, the formal campfires, the informal sing-songs. Elaborate gateways were constructed and displays of Scout talent entertained. The varied uniforms, the languages spoken, the religious tolerance shown – it was a complete spectrum of the world. Dominating at the centre of the camp was a high tower with a four-faced clock and a globe.

The royal visit

Queen Elizabeth II and the Duke of Edinburgh visited on 3 August, spending several hours touring the camp under the heat of the sun, amid crowds and dust. This was the first time that a reigning British monarch had visited a jamboree. Other distinguished visitors included the British Prime Minister, Harold Macmillan, and Sir John Hunt of Everest fame.

A pageant was enacted one afternoon in the main arena telling the story of Baden-Powell and the Scout movement by the British contingent. Baden-Powell's son, Peter, played the part of his father as an adult, and one of his grandsons played the part of young B-P. Scouts from the Charterhouse School Troop also took part.

Battling the elements

One night, the site was hit by a sudden thunderstorm that turned roads into rivers and hollows into lakes. Scouts in some parts of the site were moved to higher ground. By the following day, things returned to normal with Scouts cooking over large fires, laughing as though nothing had happened and making a nonsense of pessimistic newspaper headlines.

The closing ceremony

Monday 12 August dawned, and the last day of the Jamboree-Indaba-Moot came. In her closing speech to the participants, Olave Baden-Powell said:

'Here in this camp we are thinking more particularly today of a happy man, a man who 50 years ago, had ended an eventful career in the Army; and that end was the beginning of what we see around us today, of which this great Jamboree-Indaba-Moot and our World Camps of Guides have been but tokens – millions of boys and girls, men and women, of every colour, creed and country, living together as brothers and sisters under one Promise and one Law, that Promise and Law given to us 50 years ago by our Founder.

'He left this earth some 16 years ago and that end was indeed only a beginning. For you, too, as you come to the end of this wonderful Jamboree tonight, the end is truly only a beginning. For these two weeks you, Scouters and Scouts of so many different lands and so many different languages have lived in harmony together, forgetting all the differences which separate, and thinking only of the ties which unite you all in the great world family of Scouting.

'We celebrate our Jubilee, but it is my belief that we are at the beginning of a new era in our movement. Just as these green trees around us will soon shed their leaves in order to make room for the fresh young growth of another spring, so many of us older ones, who have come perhaps to our last World Jamboree, will make way for a new and finer and even bigger generation of Scouters and Scouts, a generation which will be finer and bigger because you who are sharing in the Jamboree today are going away determined that your efforts will make it so.'

Introducing
the Beavers

The journey of the Beavers started in Northern Ireland in 1963. 'The Little Brothers' section was launched, and they were renamed Beavers in 1966. Beavers had been one of the names B-P had considered for the Cubs.

B.E.A.V.E.R.S

The first *Beaver Handbook* was published in Northern Ireland by the Beavers Association, which was supported by The Scout Association, but remained separate. They developed a programme of activities using the word 'Beavers' as an acronym; Building, Energy Release, Adventure, Variety, Entertaining, Religion and Storytelling.

The Beaver uniform consisted of a grey jumper and an emerald green scarf. Over the course of a Beaver's two-year membership he could collect four footprint badges: green, blue, red and brown.

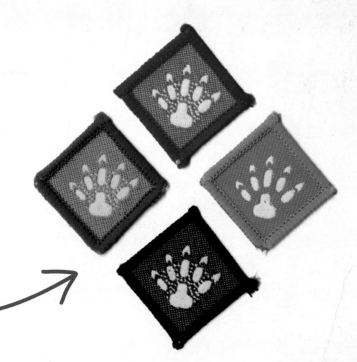

Beavers across the UK

In the mid-1970s The Scout Association looked at launching pre-Cub provision for the rest of the UK. Following the example of the Wolf Cubs almost 70 years previously, a pilot scheme was launched in 1982. During this phase, Beavers were not formal Scouts, as they did not make a Promise.

The purpose was to have fun and make friends. The initial uniform was a turquoise scarf with a maroon woggle. Many troops chose to create an informal uniform t-shirt with their name printed on it to give the members a sense of identity.

Beavers then went from strength to strength, with more than 12,000 people joining in the first year. By 1986 there were 60,000 Beavers. The Scout Association then integrated Beavers into the movement. Beaver Scouts continue to flourish, and 30 years later, they celebrated having 126,000 members.

The Beaver Handbook was first published in Northern Ireland.

The Beaver Leader's Handbook soon followed.

Scouts is a global phenomenon. United by a shared promise and common values, we are now, in the words of Bear Grylls, 'the most amazing family on Earth'. Did you know that John Lennon and David Bowie were both Scouts? Our members have gone on to do extraordinary things, from trekking to the North Pole to flying to the Moon. But the movement is at its most impressive when it is dedicated to helping others. Scouts are making a difference in their local communities, improving people's lives and bridging social and political divides.

World Scout jamborees

Celebrating the centenary

The proud tradition of World Scout Jamborees began in 1920 and continues to this day. Scouts continue to flock in their tens of thousands to these huge celebrations of international peace and friendship.

21st World Scout Jamboree

The year 2007 saw the world centenary of Scouts. It was also the first time a World Scout Jamboree has been staged in the UK since 1957. Of the many highlights, one was undoubtedly the visit from HRH Prince William who joined Scouts for the day to try activities and meet young people from across the world. The jamboree took place at Hylands Park, just outside Chelmsford, with off site locations including Gilwell Park, and Alton Water for water activities. A Sunrise Ceremony also took place on Brownsea Island to celebrate the movement's 100th birthday.

Location: Hylands Park, Chelmsford
Dates: 27 July to 8 August 2007
Attendance: 38,074, plus 50,000 day visitors
Countries represented: 158

At the Jamboree

It is 7.55am at Hylands Park on 1 August 2007. Under brilliant sunshine and on slightly damp grass, some 40,000 Scouts in the arena are waiting to become a part of history. They make up the largest gathering of Scouts in the UK for over 50 years. Only the stewards on the gate and the crews manning the radio and TV vans are not part of the huge throng waiting to celebrate the centenary.

The renewal of the Promise

As a video link up to the Sunrise Ceremony on Brownsea Island is established, a reverent hush falls on the crowd as ninth Chief Scout of the United Kingdom, Peter Duncan, blows the first of three blasts on the kudu horn, 100 years on from the first chief doing the very same thing. It is fortunate that Peter is a former trombone player!

Peter then invites the world to renew its Promise. It is a thrilling moment and across the site, Scouts hold up the familiar three-fingered Scout sign. The stage has undergone a dramatic transformation for the Sunrise Ceremony. The rainbow banners that have adorned the main stage all week have been replaced with a purple and white design featuring the dove and World Scout logo. Likewise, the flags of the world have been replaced with hundreds of World Scout flags – symbolising the powerful unity of the worldwide family.

The main stage at the 21st World Scout Jamboree, 2007.

A celebration of peace

Once the broadcast is over, the show begins, with an explosion of colour, music and dance. Yellow Sunrise scarves are whirled like football rattles over their heads – a practice that began at the opening ceremony and has grown in popularity throughout the week.

Two young people take to the stage – a French and English speaker – and introduce the show. 'Our Jamboree here is unique – Baden-Powell had a vision of a world that could live together. Here at Hylands Park, that dream has come true.' Scouts bearing the flags of the world bound on stage, before running into the crowd, much to its delight. 'Scouting has a fantastic role to play,' one of the young people says, 'and the future is in our hands. Let us prepare for peace in the world.'

At the same moment, a flock of oversized doves swoop into the crowd, guided, it transpires, on wires. But this ceremony is not all about theatrics – Scouts from all countries appear on stage to say (and sing) their own prayer for peace: 'Money does not lead to community and faith,' one says. The mood is heightened by a rousing chorus of 'One World' led by a young man with a voice for an anthem that would put Bono to shame; as it reaches its crescendo, a flock of real-live doves soar into the air; they do a quick lap of the arena, before heading off in the general direction of Chelmsford.

Prince William at the 21st World Scout Jamboree.

Lord Baden-Powell's address

A solemn fanfare signals the start of the next phase of proceedings. Lord Baden-Powell, the Founder's grandson, takes the stage with Herman Hui, Chairman of the World Scout Committee. The participants seemed impressed with this direct link to the Founder and his clear, informal address is warmly received: 'I am very happy to be with you this morning,' he says. 'My grandfather started this movement; he wanted young people to discover new things and learn how to look after themselves. Now millions of people are doing the same thing. The movement he started has been one of the world's most powerful instruments for international peace.'

He concludes, movingly, with a message from his grandfather: 'The real way to happiness is to give happiness to other people,' he reads. 'Stick to your Scout Promise always and may God help you to do it. Your friend, Baden-Powell.'

A positive reaction

'I liked the part when all the flags came on,' said Sebastian from Denmark. 'The best bit was the doves flying,' says Peter from Hungary. Marbin from the Philippines was impressed by the whole event: 'The link up to Brownsea Island was amazing with the whole world embracing peace. The grandson's speech was really great.' David, meanwhile, a Scout and musician from Washington State, was more impressed by the sound system – 'I liked the show and everything, but that was a really nice bass!'

'The future is in our hands.'
Robert Baden-Powell

22nd World Scout Jamboree

On the coast of Sweden, the 22nd World Scout Jamboree took place in an idyllic rural location adorned with pine trees – in keeping with its theme of 'Simply Scouting,' focusing on the outdoors and traditional skills.

The sight of Bear Grylls abseiling down to the stage at the opening of the 22nd World Scout Jamboree is one that few of the participants will forget. As the outdoors is such a big part of life in Sweden, this was bound to be reflected in the theme, which focused on Simply Scouting and the three key components of meetings, nature and solidarity.

Despite a huge amount of rain across the Jamboree, it relented for the ceremony itself on the evening of 28 July. On behalf of the UK, hosts of the previous Jamboree, Bear Grylls, UK Chief Scout, handed over the World Scout Flag to the organisers of the 22nd World Scout Jamboree. A Promise renewal, dancing and singing followed – including a rousing rendition of the jamboree song.

Other ceremonies were equally spectacular. The lighthouse ceremony on 30 July was an interfaith gathering with contributions from all religious denominations represented. Meanwhile the Mid Event saw skydivers swooping down near the main arena clutching jamboree flags. Live music and a dirt bike display capped a memorable day. Perhaps the best was saved until last. The closing ceremony on 7 August featured a spectacular firework display, video flashbacks and a speech by the Secretary General of World Scouting.

The UK contingent at the 22nd World Scout Jamboree in Sweden.

Location: Rankaby, Kristianstad, Scania, Sweden
Dates: 27 July to 7 August 2011
Attendance: 40,061
Countries represented: 166

23rd World
Scout Jamboree

'A Spirit of Unity' was the theme for this extraordinary gathering in the west of Japan during summer 2015. To give a sense of the size and scale, an arena, a hospital and two supermarkets were specially built for the event.

The varied programme including not just adventurous activities from wind surfing to sand biking, but community events, too. Perhaps the most powerful moment came when Scouts from each contingent took part in a ceremony to mark the 70th anniversary of the bombing of Hiroshima and Nagasaki.

International friendship

At the Scouts, international friendship and co-operation comes as second nature, something a World Scout Jamboree underlines time and again. But how do we rise to the challenge of providing opportunities for all young people to work towards a more peaceful world?

For those who have never attended a World Scout Jamboree, what strikes you first is the sheer scale of it. Some 35,000 people attended this time from 150 different countries. The UK sent the largest delegation of over 3,000 young people who experienced the adventure of a lifetime and a truly life-changing fortnight, thanks to the incredible efforts of over 1,000 volunteers.

Location: Kirarahama, Yamaguchi, Japan
Dates: 28 July to 8 August 2015
Attendance: 33,628
Countries represented: 150

the cultural awareness and literacy that is needed for young people to navigate and make their mark on the world. This is why the jamboree and wider Scouting events, such as the Moot, Roverway and international expeditions, are so critically important.

More that unites us than divides us

The international nature of the Scouts is such an important part of the movement. Scouts have a duty to make sure that youth members are not just active citizens, but are global citizens too, and are able to see that, whatever your nationality, there is more that unites us than divides us.

Through the delivery of the programme, and opening up more international experiences, Scouts can foster

As Baden-Powell said at the first World Scout Jamboree, 'differences exist between the peoples of the world in thought and sentiment, just as they do in language and physique. The jamboree has taught us that if we exercise mutual forbearance and give and take, then there is sympathy and harmony. If it be your will, let us go forth from here fully determined that we will develop among ourselves... that comradeship... so that we may help to develop peace and happiness in the world.' That sentiment is as true today as it was in 1920.

A spirit of unity

As well as the scale of the event, what was as extraordinary was the way young people from different countries shared stories and forged friendships united by shared Scout values. Many Scouts found it particularly moving to visit Hiroshima 70 years after the devastation of the atomic bomb.

To see the impact on those inspiring young people as they reflected on the events was something unforgettable.

All around the sub camps, there were people from all nationalities sharing food, singing, laughing together and pledging to stay in touch and co-operate in the future.

Pushing
frontiers

Adventurous Scouts

From Karen Darke handcycling across Patagonia to Sean Conway swimming from Lands End to John O'Groats, Scouts have a proud tradition of going the extra mile.

From Arch to Arctic /// Robert McArthur and Poldy van Lynden

In 2018, Robert McArthur and Poldy van Lynden ran, swam, cycled and rowed 5,000 kilometres from London's Marble Arch to the Arctic island of Svalbard to raise money for the Scouts.

The two adventurers ran three marathons, swam the English Channel and cycled through seven countries from Calais to Tromso before a five-day, 1126-kilometre (700-mile) row to the Arctic Circle at Longyearbyen, on the island of Svalbard. They completed the entire trip by human power alone.

Prior to training for his epic Arch2Arctic challenge, Robert McArthur had never participated in traditional triathlon sports. However, he now enjoys regular 20- to 30-kilometre runs and 70- to 100-kilometre bike rides, and he completed the 17-kilometre Windermere swim in challenging conditions.

Poldy van Lynden was a keen runner before Arch2Arctic, completing the London Marathon and other long distance challenges. He also cycled 20 kilometres each day and swam the length of Lake Windermere.

The toughest part of the challenge for Poldy was the channel swim, which took him a gruelling 18 hours. It was the closest he came to giving up. 'I couldn't lift one of my shoulders and it was the most exhausted I'd ever been. The tide actually should have swept me back out to sea – the pilot said he had never seen it do that before, so luck was clearly on my side.'

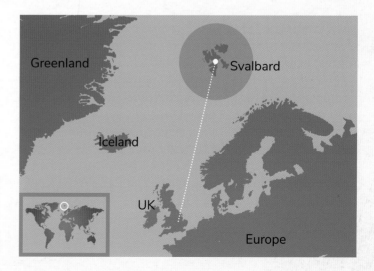

Patagonia and beyond /// Karen Darke

Karen is a gold-medal-winning Paralympic hand cyclist and adventurer. She has crossed the Greenland ice cap on skis, handcycled across Patagonia and won gold in handcycling in Rio, 2016. Despite suffering a serious accident in her early twenties, Karen has continued to live a life of adventure.

'As an ex-climber, I often hear about climbers doing the seven summits – the highest summit on each continent. I decided to create a hand biking alternative. I'm completing nine major hand biking routes, across all seven continents.

'I'm pleased I've been able to live such a full, active life with my disability. Because I was always adventurous by nature, I think I've taken it for granted at times. Not everybody living with a disability pursues the kinds of things I have. Many people aren't able to, and I've been very fortunate. Getting into the Paralympics was obviously a really proud moment; winning silver at the 2012 London games, and gold at the Rio games in 2016. I know how much hard work it's taken to get here, so it's quite special.

'I think Scouting imbues that sense of adventure and shows young people that there is a wider world out there for them. You don't always get that opportunity through your parents or school. Scouting is another route to take, another route to opportunity. It helps you build belief in yourself, and to work in a team with others. These are all skills that are important in everyday life.'

Walking the Amazon /// Ed Stafford

Explorer and former Cub and Scout Ed Stafford is a world record holder for the longest ever jungle expedition. Today, Ed is a proud UK Scout Ambassador.

Ed became the first person ever to have walked the length of the Amazon River, completing this epic feat on 9 August 2010. This was more than two years on from when he set off on 2 April 2008 in the south of Peru. Ed finished the expedition with the help of the guide, Gadiel 'Cho' Sánchez Rivera.

Ed's next challenge was even more extreme – being marooned on an island in the Pacific for 60 days without food, water or equipment.

Swimming the length of Britain /// Sean Conway

In 2013, Sean Conway completed the incredible feat of swimming the length of Britain – from Land's End to John O'Groats. In 2016, he also finished an epic 6,750-kilometre (4,200-mile) odyssey around the coast of Britain.

'I think swimming the length of Britain was my hardest challenge. For the most part people ignored me, laughed at me or tried to stop me. It wasn't just a question of swimming ability, it was organising the logistics that proved most challenging. Fortunately, there were people who truly believed in me, and I repaid that faith by completing the challenge.'

Sean's great-uncle was Sir Charles Warren, who was instrumental in the beginnings of the Scouts with Baden-Powell: 'I have a special connection with the movement in that my great-uncle, Sir Charles Warren, helped Baden-Powell start the Scouts way back in the early years of the 20th century. He fought in the Boer War with him and when they were both back in England, Sir Charles gave B-P some advice. He started one of the very first Scout groups himself, the 1st St. Lawrence in Kent, which thrives to this day.

'What the Scouts do is so valuable. It teaches you resilience, thinking on your feet and leadership. It gives you the character to keep going when it's cold and wet, as well as key skills like map reading.'

To cap it all, in April 2019, Sean completed the London Marathon dressed as a giant Scout badge.

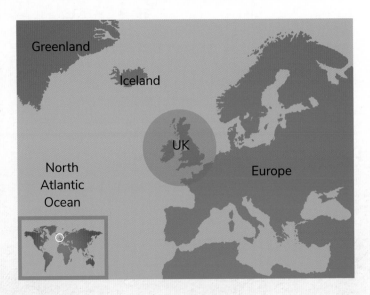

On top of the world /// Dwayne Fields

Best known for being the first black Briton to walk to the North Pole, Dwayne is also a former Cub Scout and an advocate of the power of Scouts to help young people develop skills for life.

Born in Jamaica, Dwayne arrived in the UK at the age of six. He grew up in north and east London and was a victim of knife and gun crime, narrowly escaping a street shooting before deciding to forge a new path in life.

'I re-evaluated who I was, I looked at what I wanted to achieve and I asked myself what would make my great-grandmother proud.'

He went on to complete a combined honours degree in psychology, international development and business management and spent three years as an electrical mechanical engineer for the London Underground before following his passion and raising funds to reach the North Pole. In 2013, Dwayne was awarded the Freedom of the City of London. He hopes he can use his position to encourage more inner-city young people to get out into nature.

'Getting people outdoors brings people together and together they learn interpersonal skills, teamwork skills and planning skills. We spend so much of our lives online or immersed in our work or just segregated, that we're losing crucial skills. Scouting can offer young people all of these skills.'

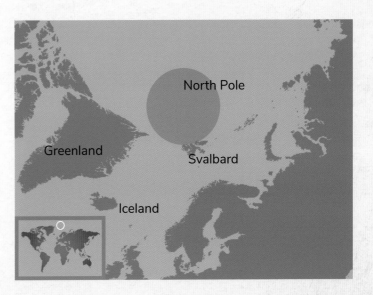

Scouts in space

UK Scout Ambassador and ESA Astronaut Tim Peake is not the first Scout to venture into space. Scouts have a long history of using their skills to go above and beyond...

Neil Armstrong

It's 20 July 1969 and a Scout is about to set foot on the Moon. It's the culmination of an astonishing journey that took Neil Armstrong from a bright-eyed young Scout in Ohio, to fighter ace in the Korean War, to test pilot and engineer, and finally to NASA

astronaut. Neil was an inaugural member of Troop 25 in Sandusky, Ohio, which was formed in 1941 in the wake of the attack on Pearl Harbour. After three happy years in Wolf Patrol, engaged in the usual range of outdoor pursuits, as well as raising money for the war effort, he moved with his family to Wapakoneta a little further south.

Neil earns his wings

Keen to continue his journey as a Scout, he joined Troop 14, where he busied himself building model aircraft and improving his knowledge of astronomy and aeronautics. Excelling in almost everything he did (he earned 26 merit badges instead of the required 21), it came as no surprise to his peers that he went on to become an Eagle Scout, the highest distinction for any young person in US Scouting.

Neil went on to repay his debt to the Scouts in a number of unique ways. The first, and most

extraordinary, was that he took a World Membership Badge with him to the Moon. The badge is now in the safekeeping of the World Organization of the Scout Movement, along with a letter of authenticity: 'I certify that this World Scout Badge was carried on the surface of the moon on man's first lunar landing, Apollo XI, July 20 1969.'

In turn, the Scouts were keen to claim Neil as their own. On his return to Earth, Neil became a recipient of the coveted Silver Buffalo Award for extraordinary service to young people.

Strange but true

There is an extraordinary postscript to Neil's story. Years after the moon landing, a 17-year-old Scout named Ken Dayton was attempting his Space Exploration Badge, but had hit an obstacle: no certified adjudicator could be found to sign it off.

Joking, his leader suggested he find an astronaut to do the job. Taking this instruction literally, Dayton drove the 240 kilometres (150 miles) to Armstrong's farm in Ohio and put in his request. Clearly inspired by the Scout's dedication and tenacity, Armstrong listened attentively for half an hour while Dayton gave his presentation in Armstrong's driveway. As thorough as ever, Neil Armstrong asked the young Scout to send his file of evidence to his university office for a final inspection. He then issued this statement:

'Scout Ken Dayton has appeared before me to demonstrate his completion of the Space Exploration Badge. I am not a certified counselor and cannot legally affirm Mr Dayton's competence… In my opinion, he has completed all requirements satisfactorily.'

NATIONAL AERONAUTICS AND SPACE ADMINISTRATION
MANNED SPACECRAFT CENTER
HOUSTON, TEXAS 77058

I certify that this World Scout Badge was carried to the surface of the moon on man's first lunar landing, Apollo XI, July 20, 1969.

Neil A. Armstrong
Crew Commander
Apollo XI

Tim Peake, Scout Ambassador

A former Cub Scout, Tim went on to spend 186 days on the International Space Station (ISS) and is now a UK Scout Ambassador.

Born in 1972 and schooled in Chichester, West Sussex, Tim went on to Sandhurst in 1990. He beat over 9,000 other applicants for one of the six places on the European Space Agency's new astronaut training programme. He was launched to the ISS in December 2015 and participated in the first spacewalk outside the ISS by a British astronaut in January 2016. In April that year, he ran the London Marathon from the ISS treadmill.

'Scouting started me on an incredible journey. As a Cub Scout, I never dreamed that someday I would be looking at our beautiful planet from space. I went from spending nights under the stars to spending nights among the stars.'

In summer 2018, Tim Peake made a surprise appearance to a group of Hampshire Scouts working on their Astronautics badge. He helped them build water rockets and took part in a question and answer session about life on the International Space Station.

'Scouting set me on the right path at a young age because I loved the outdoors and I loved adventure. It gave me the opportunity to discover new interests, explore new boundaries and build the confidence to achieve new goals. Scouting was the first step on a journey that led to me becoming an astronaut. With the right people, the right attitude and the right skills, anything is possible.'

> **'I went from spending nights under the stars to spending nights among the stars.'**
>
> Tim Peake, Scout Ambassador

> **'Scouts was the first step on a journey that led to me becoming an astronaut. With the right skills, anything is possible.'**
>
> Tim Peake, Scout Ambassador

Scouts flying high

Since the start of the US space program in 1959, out of the 320 pilots and scientists that have been selected by NASA, an amazing 181 of them were Scouts.

Of the 24 men to travel to the Moon on the Apollo, 20 were Scouts, including 11 of the 12 moonwalkers, and all three members of the crew of Apollo 13 were Scouts. Three Scout astronauts have travelled to the Moon twice. But these great feats of exploration came at a cost. All three of the astronauts who died in the Apollo I fire, four of the seven who died in the space shuttle Challenger, and five of the seven who died in the space shuttle Columbia were Scouts.

In the USA today, Scouts who earn the prestigious Eagle Scout Award and Girl Scouts who earn the Gold Award can receive a congratulatory letter and certificate of recognition from NASA commemorating their distinguished achievement.

Scouts and royalty

A royal connection

The Scout movement's links with royalty go back almost to the very beginning. In the winter of 1909 – two years on from the camp on Brownsea Island – King Edward VII gave the Scouts his royal approval when B-P stayed at Balmoral in Scotland.

Support from the throne

In 1911 King Edward VII's son, George V, approved the grant of Scouting's Royal Charter, which gave legal protection to the Scout movement. At George VI's coronation in May 1937, Scouts were once again centre stage. Needless to say, Scouts supported the young Queen when she acceded to the throne in 1952, ushering in a new age of youthful optimism.

A young Princess Elizabeth reviews Scouts in the 1930s.

Queen Elizabeth II and the Scouts

1931
On 10 June, Princess Elizabeth helps the president of the Scouts – her great-uncle, the Duke of Connaught – inspect a Troop.

1937
Princess Elizabeth becomes a Guide and Princess Margaret joins as a Brownie.

Princess Elizabeth attends the National Parade of King's Scouts at Windsor (the only National Scout Service parade attended by Robert Baden-Powell).

1952
Queen Elizabeth reviews the National Parade of Queen's Scouts at Windsor Castle and takes the salute for the first time.

1953
Scouts assist the crowds at the Coronation of Queen Elizabeth II.

The Queen accepts the Gold Wolf.

1954
The Queen attends a Gang Show at Golders Green Hippodrome, London.

1957
At the 1957 World Scout Jamboree, Indaba and Moot, The Queen is received as a VIP.

1961
Baden-Powell House, South Kensington, is opened by Queen Elizabeth II as a living monument to the Founder.

1968
Prince Andrew, the Queen's second son, joins 1st Marylebone Cub Scout Pack; for the duration of his membership, the Pack meets at Buckingham Palace.

1972
The Queen and Duke of Edinburgh attend the 40th anniversary production of Ralph Reader's Gang Show.

1975
The Duke of Kent is appointed President of the Scouts by the Queen.

1976
The Queen formally opens the new Scout Headquarters at Baden-Powell House.

The Queen names an RNLI lifeboat *The Scout* in Hartlepool.

1977
Scouts across the UK celebrate the Queen's Silver Jubilee – and wear a commemorative badge.

1982
Royal visit to Hawkhirst Adventure Camp (now Scout Adventures, Hawkhirst).

1995
The Queen visits Gilwell Park to reopen the White House and refurbished training centre.

2002
Queen's Scouts assist at the lying in state of the Queen Elizabeth, the Queen Mother.

In June, 120 Scouts take part in the Queen's Golden Jubilee celebrations in London.

2007
The Queen reviews the Parade of Queen's Scouts at Windsor during the centenary year.

2008
The Queen meets Scouts and unveils a bronze bust at Baden-Powell House, South Kensington.

Queen and country

In the early days, the Queen was a figurehead for all Scouts in the Commonwealth. She continues to take a strong interest in the growth and development of the movement throughout the world.

The Queen and Scouts worldwide

The Scout movement, like HM the Queen, has travelled the world. Wherever she goes, no matter how far, Scouts are always a familiar face and welcome her.

From her 1953 visit to Auckland, New Zealand, where 16,000 young people greeted her in her coronation year, to visits to tiny islands, like St Vincent, in the Windward Islands, she is always cheered by their loyalty and enthusiasm.

A Cub Scout meets the Queen in Windsor, 2007.

The Queen opens Baden-Powell House in South Kensington, London.

'At Scouts I've had the opportunity to try out loads of new activities and gain new skills. Meeting the Queen has been one of the best adventures yet.'

Amy Brundson, Explorer Scout, who met the Queen at Baden-Powell House in 2008

Out for a royal occasion

On a rainy June morning in 1953, Scouts were out on the streets of London, distributing programmes and helping the crowds of people who had camped out for the night. *The King and I* was playing in the West End, and for ladies, the Audrey Hepburn look was in, with tight waistlines and bunched hair. In the East End, double-breasted suits were dusted off for the day and school boys and girls wore blazers and buttoned duffel coats over v-neck jumpers. Union Jacks fluttered on every street in numbers not seen since VE Day, all for the coronation of the young Queen.

Nearly 60 years on, Scouts lined the streets again, at the wedding of the Duke and Duchess of Cambridge (and it's still raining). In 2012, Scouts were out again as the Queen celebrated her Diamond Jubilee.

The Queen's Diamond Jubilee badge that was worn by Scouts and Guides throughout 2012.

King and Scout

His Majesty, the King of Sweden, Carl XVI Gustaf, has played an active role in World Scouting for most of his life.

Having joined the Scouts more than 50 years ago, HM the King of Sweden strongly believes that the movement is still relevant to young people.

On the role of Scouting in modern society, he said: 'society still has problems we need to deal with and through Scouting young people can play a constructive role in society and help in their communities.'

Speaking at the 21st World Scout Jamboree, he said: 'To be at a big event like this, where kids have fun and make a lot of new friends, having here more than 150 nations, it's just fantastic!'

The King of Sweden is one of few who have been awarded the Bronze Wolf, the highest distinction of the World Organisation of the Scout movement, for exceptional services to World Scouting.

Royal volunteer

The evening of 14 December 2016 is one that Cub Scouts in Kings Lynn are not likely to forget. They were joined by HRH the Duchess of Cambridge.

A great supporter of the Scouts, the Duchess previously volunteered with a Cub Scout Pack when she lived in Anglesey, North Wales. She has visited a number of Scout events over the years.

During her visit to Kings Lynn, Norfolk, the Duchess helped volunteers run a variety of skills-based activities. To start the evening in true Cub fashion, she led some classic parachute games, designed to develop teamwork and cooperation.

The Cubs also learned First Aid, creative cake decorating and looked at ways to maintain good mental wellbeing. After a mass singalong of Happy Birthday, the duchess cut a special 100th birthday

cake and even decorated her own Cub cupcake. To top off the evening's celebrations, the Duchess recited the Cub Scout Promise along with the Cubs.

Cub Scout Leader, Hazel Coley, was ecstatic to have the opportunity to show the duchess around and said, 'Meeting the Duchess has been the best birthday present this Cub Scout Pack could have possibly imagined. It's an evening that they will never forget, and the most exciting thing that has happened to me in all my time as a volunteer. The duchess helped our Cub Scouts learn valuable skills and that's what the Scouts is all about, adults and young people alike having fun, enjoying new adventures and learning new skills.'

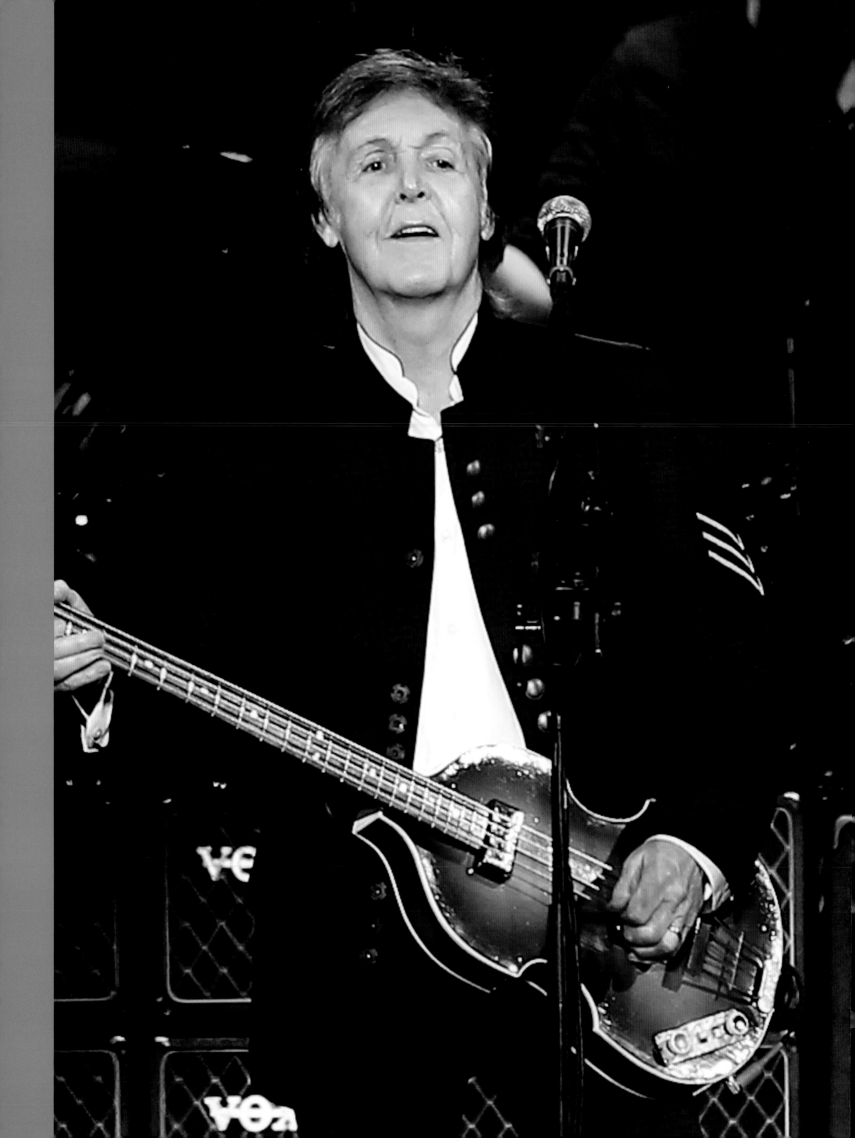

Inspirational Scouts

Rock 'n' roll Scouts

From campfire songs to performing for crowds of thousands, several world-famous singers and musicians were members of the Scout movement in their younger years.

David Bowie

The young David Robert Jones brought the same sense of style to his Scout Troop that was later recognisable in Ziggy Stardust. His first musical performance was at a Scout camp on the Isle of Wight in 1958. David accompanied his friend George on the ukulele, while George played washboard bass and sang. Perhaps Bowie also got his love of dressing up from those days.

Taylor Swift

The pop-country sensation was once a Girl Scout. She must have learned a thing or two about good turns, as Taylor has contributed to numerous diverse causes, from children's literacy to cancer research. No stranger to charity concerts and benefits, in 2012, Swift was recognised with a Kid's Choice Big Help Award.

Jarvis Cocker, Pulp

Sheffield's favourite son was a Scout before he formed Pulp. When their album *Different Class* went on to sell more than a million copies, Jarvis donated the platinum disc to his old Scout group in Sheffield, UK, which was then auctioned to help them raise funds for a new headquarters.

Keith Richards, The Rolling Stones

The seemingly indestructible rocker credits the Scouts for nurturing the leadership skills that helped him form a band. In *Life* (2010), his autobiography, Keith wrote: 'I got to be Patrol Leader within six weeks – I just shot to the top [...] Once I had a bunch of guys together, it doesn't matter if it was the Scouts or a band, I could see my way clear to pull all their various talents together.'

Jim Morrison, The Doors

The famous frontman of The Doors was a Cub Scout in the Boy Scouts of America. The American Indian influences of Den meetings may even have sparked his interest in mystical lore and spirituality, which went on to inform many of his lyrics and poems. Today, Jim Morrison's old Cub Scout uniform is exhibited at the Rock 'n' Roll Hall of Fame in Cleveland, Ohio.

Mariah Carey

America's favourite singer joined the Girl Scouts while growing up on Long Island. It might be hard to imagine her singing around a campfire, but she certainly has an outdoor spirit. She has set up Camp Mariah, a Fresh Air Fund-operated summer camp in Fishkill, New York State to help disadvantaged, inner-city youths. She is also a major benefactor of the Make-A-Wish Foundation.

Twist and Scout

The Scout story is full of surprises. Not least is that John Lennon and Paul McCartney, probably the greatest songwriters of the 20th century, both started out in the Scouts.

At the Scout camp

The next time you sing 'Yellow Submarine' around the campfire you might want to share the Scouting story that led to its creation. In his 2008 Grammy-nominated song 'That Was Me', Paul McCartney takes a nostalgic look back at scenes from his extraordinary life. 'That was me, at the Scout camp' he sings in the first line, giving a clue to how fresh Scouting still is in his memory. In fact, it's possible to identify which trip he's referring to: a camp in July 1957 at Hathersage in Derbyshire which he attended with his brother Mike (later Mike McGear of The Scaffold).

Memories of Lennon

John Lennon, the wit behind such songs as 'I Am The Walrus' and 'Strawberry Fields Forever', was once a member of the 3rd Allerton Scout Group. The Cubs met in St Peter's Church Hall, the very place where John first met Paul on 6 July 1957.

Darren Suttle, a leader at the group, interviewed his predecessor, David Ashton, who knew John. 'John Lennon turned up at Cubs and later at Scouts from time to time,' David recalls. 'I remember him being at Scout Sports at Allerton and the Scout Swimming Gala at Garston Baths, but mostly he met up for the normal Scout meetings with their easy-going, relaxed atmosphere. We called ourselves The Backwoods Men.'

It seems that John enjoyed the best sort of Scouting – frequent trips out of the city and into the countryside. 'We prided ourselves in being able to live off the land,' says David. 'Going camping and leaving the campsite as though no-one had been there. We had summer camps on farms for two weeks in North Wales and the Lake District and also weekend camps at Graces Farm near Cronton at Easter, Whitsun and in the autumn.'

Influencing music

The influence of this early contact with nature is easy to spot in their work. Paul's 'Mother Nature's Son' and 'Blackbird', both from 'The Beatles' (more commonly known as 'The White Album') evoke idealised rural idylls, as does the original version of John's 'Jealous Guy', which started life as 'Child of Nature'. It was a theme they would return to throughout their careers, from Paul's 'Heart of the Country', 'Country Dreamer' and 'Jenny Wren', to John's 'Norwegian Wood', 'Across the Universe' and 'Free as a Bird'.

Paul evidently enjoyed these early days. 'I was a Scout, but I didn't get many badges – I got a bivouac badge for camping out.' His attentions were already turning to music and he was, by his own admission, a more diligent school pupil than John.

Role models

One of the experiences John and Paul shared was the loss of their mothers at an early age. John lost his mother Julia twice – once when she handed him over to be fostered by her sister, Mimi, and again when Julia was run over by a drunk driver.

'The men were just invisible in my family,' said John, 'I was always with the women.' With an absent father, perhaps the leaders he encountered in Scouting provided the missing male role models he needed. It's a sentiment with which David agrees: 'I think the [leaders] played a very important role in John Lennon's formative years, as they certainly did in mine.'

Paul McCartney (third row up, second left) with his Cub Scout Pack in Liverpool. Believe it or not, Paul McCartney missed his first scheduled gig with John Lennon and the Quarrymen (the band they were both in before The Beatles) because of the Scouts. The gig was at the Cavern Club on 7 August 1957 – but Paul and his brother were away at Scout camp in Hathersage, Derbyshire, at the time. Sometimes Scouts just has to come first...

A musical education

But it wasn't just camping tips that John picked up from his Scout group. It also formed a key part of his musical education. One gift his mother had given him was teaching him some chords on the banjo, which he then transferred onto a guitar. He developed this interest further in his Scout Troop.

'John's Scout Leader, Bill Whiteside, had a brother, Charlie, who lived near Penny Lane,' recounts David. 'Charlie could play chords on a banjo and we often had a campfire sing-song. I remember making nettle soup and bread twists on sticks while Charlie taught John the chords to "Way Down Upon the Swanee River".' He also got to perfect his skills on the mouth organ, which was later to feature prominently on such early Beatles' hits as 'Love Me Do' and 'From Me to You'. The boys had learned to sing the song 'The Happy Wanderer', which John Lennon soon mastered on his 'mouthy'. This tune obviously stuck in his mind.

'I used to embarrass authority by chanting out a weird version of "The Happy Wanderer",' John later recalled. 'I daydreamed my way through school. I wasn't there – I was at the movies or running around.'

Peace and love

Did Scouting influence them on a more fundamental level? In many ways, Scout values anticipated the notions of universal peace and love that would become so popular in the 1960s. The clothes may have been very different, but the sentiment of loving your neighbour, doing good turns and spreading a message of international peace and universal happiness are strikingly similar.

Face to face with the Chief

John Lennon is also said to have met the Chief Scout himself. 'We once went to a Scout campsite near Ormskirk,' says David. 'There was great excitement as we were to meet the Chief Scout. We set up camp for the 3rd Allerton Scouts all on our own without any leaders and the Chief Scout came and talked to us all personally.

'I remember John being at that camp, as he was in our patrol, the Badgers. He helped me carry a milk churn full of water back to our campsite in the woods.'

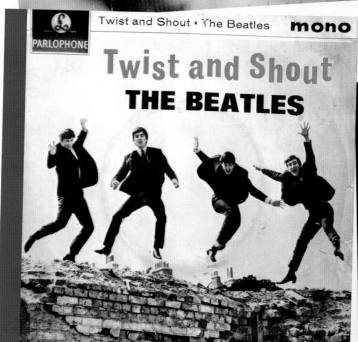

High-flying Scouts

Scouts have gone on to become presidents, astronauts, Olympians, film stars and entrepreneurs. Here are some of their thoughts on the Scout movement.

'The international Scout movement is a world leader in youth education and has particular relevance to the needs of youth in Africa and the emerging democracies around the globe. I am pleased with the progress of Scouting in South Africa, and in the steps which are now being taken to make the program accessible to more young people. The importance of a high moral code, which is at the foundation of the Scout movement, cannot be stressed too highly.'

Nelson Mandela

Former President of South Africa

'Scouting got me away from the desk, got me doing useful, fun and exciting things. Thinking back, it taught me more things than school ever did. Great fun, great adventures. Lots of outdoor activities, which I love. Experience of leadership. Never could learn how to tie a knot though!'

Sir Richard Branson

Entrepreneur

'I actually like snakes! When I was young, I was a Scout nature camp counselor, and one of our projects was collecting snakes and creating an environment for them, so I'm quite familiar with snakes and think they're fantastic creatures.'

Harrison Ford

Actor

'Young people need positive role models. They also need a safe, nurturing and supportive environment where they can try new things and not be afraid to fail. Scouting is one of those places.'

Ellie Simmonds

Paralympic gold medallist

'I have really fond memories of being a Cub Scout. I was particularly proud of being made a sixer. It was such a proud moment for me. I'm really happy now to encourage others to join, learn skills and have the same positive experience. I am grateful for what Scouting did for me.'

Warwick Davis

Actor

'I remember my time as a Wolf Cub very well indeed. We learned a lot of useful things and had a great deal of fun.'

Sir David Attenborough

Broadcaster and naturalist

'I was one of the first females in our Cub Scout Pack. It led to a love of the outdoors and really grew my confidence. The confidence that you gain through Scouting is something that you just can't buy.'

Helen Glover

Olympic gold medallist

'I strongly believe in Scouting. It's a source of great strength to us.'

John F. Kennedy

Former president of the United States of America

'For a century Scouts have served their nation and communities in ways both large and small. Some of our nation's greatest heroes have worn the Scout uniform. Today, Scouts improve our neighbourhoods and reach out to those less fortunate and that service is worth celebrating.'

Barack Obama

Former president of the United States of America

Bear Grylls: Leading the way

Meet the Chief

Bear Grylls is the UK Chief Scout and the first ever Chief Ambassador of World Scouting. He is the inspirational volunteer leader of a movement of 640,000 members across the UK and 50 million around the world.

A young Chief

Appointed in 2009 at the age of 34, Bear was the youngest person to hold the role of Chief Scout. Bear has overseen a period of unprecedented growth and expansion in the movement in the UK. Such was his popularity with young people, adult volunteers and the public, Bear was reappointed in April 2015 as UK Chief Scout so that he could continue his mission to bring Scouting to all.

Inspiring others

The Scouts provides fun, friendship and skills for life to more than 460,000 young people and 160,000 adults in the UK alone, making it the UK's largest coeducational youth movement. It helps girls and boys, young men and women aged six to 25, develop the skills and values they need to succeed in life.

Bear's great strength is inspiring people to go beyond the ordinary and stretch themselves to discover new skills, talents and qualities. He has also engendered a spirit of positivity, kindness and generosity in the movement, leading by example. He describes Scouts as 'shining lights in their communities'.

Energy and optimism

Every organisation reflects its leader, and Bear's energy and positivity can be seen across the movement. He has inspired hundreds of thousands of young people to look to the future with optimism and become active citizens in their local, national and international communities.

As a volunteering role model, Bear has talked of the advantages of flexible volunteering in people's lives, highlighting the significant personal development opportunities. Bear is committed to Scouting for all and has helped children from all backgrounds and communities to benefit from Scouting.

He has called the Scouts 'a character factory' helping young people develop resilience, determination, 'grit', independence and social, team and leadership skills that will make a powerful difference to their lives. He also underlines the importance of outdoor adventure, warning of the dangers of sedentary lifestyles – it's all about balancing screen time with green time.

Attending the 22nd World Scout Jamboree in Sweden in 2011 and visiting many groups abroad, Bear has promoted international peace, friendship and cooperation among the world's 50 million Scouts.

Inspiring youth social action

In 2016, Bear launched A Million Hands, a campaign to provide opportunities for young people to tackle four of the biggest issues facing society today. Scouts helped improve the lives of those affected by dementia, the disabled, and have improved the mental well-being and resilience of families, ensuring everyone has access to clean water and sanitation. In response to Bear's call to action, over 250,000 young people pledged their support to the cause.

Bear in the Air

Since 2009, Bear has travelled to more than 30 large-scale Scout camps in the UK, meeting over 200,000 members, taking part in activities alongside them, teaching skills and providing encouragement. These 'Bear in the Air' events are highlights of the Scouting year.

Chief Scout's Awards

A significant part of the Chief Scout's role is celebrating young people's achievements. The Chief Scout's Award is the highest award in each of the youth sections in the UK. Since 2009, hundreds of thousands of awards have been given out, helping young people to realise their potential, complete expeditions, work in their community and develop new skills. Each year, Bear attends the annual awards ceremony at Windsor Castle and personally congratulates young achievers, including recipients of the prestigious Queen's Scout Award.

The Community Impact Staged Activity Badge.

Message from the Chief Scout

'When I became Chief Scout, it was one of the proudest moments of my life. And with every passing day since then I have become ever more inspired by the tireless dedication that our leaders and volunteers put in to preparing our young people with skills for life.

From huge jamborees to a Beaver Scout enjoying a brilliant programme on a Tuesday night, every moment of Scouting is so precious. Together we build positive memories for thousands of young people and endeavour to equip them with skills for life.

Together we have grown our movement, helped other people in our communities, given young people the voice they deserve and welcomed so many new communities to Scouting. It's all about delivering chances to young people where they are needed most.

My role as Chief Ambassador for World Scouting is about bringing adventure and life skills to young people not just in the UK but all around the world as well. We are all part of this global Scouting family, this force for good, some 50 million Scouts strong.

Today my goal remains the same: to encourage and stand up for you and our young people in all we do. To show the value of courage and kindness and never giving up.'

Bear Grylls

UK Scout ambassadors

UK Scout Ambassadors help raise national awareness of the Scouts' work helping young people develop skills for life. They raise the profile and extend the reach of the Scouts across the UK.

Megan Hine
Adventurer and survival expert

Bear Grylls
Chief Scout

Tim Peake
ESA astronaut

Julia Bradbury
TV presenter

In the UK, a dedicated team of Scout Ambassadors are spreading the word. These volunteers have visited camps, led skills masterclasses and spoken about the Scouts in the media. They have inspired thousands of Scouts and volunteers. Tim Peake even helped answer calls in the Scout Information Centre!

They all credit Scouts with giving young people confidence, determination and the power of believing in themselves. When ambassadors such as DJ Chris Evans tell millions of listeners that we need volunteers, it really helps bring in new members.

One of the most memorable moments was when Steve Backshall and Helen Glover took 20 Scouts and Explorers into the wild in the Lake District in August 2017. The pair led the Scouts through 24 hours of shelter building and outdoor cooking, with an epic paddling race across Lake Windermere. The adventure culminated in a 490-metre (1,600-foot) ascent of the Old Man of Coniston.

See pages 158 to 159 for more Scout Ambassadors: Ellie Simmonds, Paralympic swimming gold medallist; Helen Glover, Olympic rowing gold medallist; and Warwick Davis, actor and director.

'The Scouts help young people get the best possible start in life.'

Megan Hine, Scout Ambassador

Ed Stafford
Explorer and TV presenter

Dwayne Fields
Polar explorer

Steve Backshall
Naturalist, adventurer and TV presenter

Anita Rani
Journalist and broadcaster

Scouts today: Changing the world

Preparing for
the future

Today, almost half a million Scouts in the UK, and more than 50 million worldwide, enjoy fun, friendship and outdoor adventure. They develop a sense of optimism and strong values as well as the leadership and teamwork skills that are more valuable than ever.

Bringing society together

Society is changing. In often fragmented communities, the pressures and expectations on young people are increasing. The future is uncertain. Scouts has never been so important in helping young people prepare for the future, developing the skills they need to succeed in a changing world.

With recent shifts in local and global politics, in many ways, society has rarely felt more divided in our lifetimes. When the world feels more inward-facing, Scouting has a more powerful role to play, bringing communities together.

Across the globe, we're seeing young people calling for more inclusive, kinder communities. Youth movements are campaigning for better, more affordable education, for more tolerant communities, for a world that better reflects the diversity of who we are. The younger generations really are very community oriented.

By continuing to close the gaps between people and generations, we're building stronger, happier, more cohesive communities...

... across divided communities

Scouts brings people together. We offer shared experiences and a place to meet those from different backgrounds, promoting mutual understanding and building friendships.

... in times of uncertainty

Scouts helps young people develop the values, self-belief and belief in others that will help them become confident, active citizens. We offer a place to belong, skills to succeed and are optimistic about the future.

... lack of community engagement

Scouts gives young people opportunities to improve the lives of those around them, taking positive social action in their local, national and international communities.

... in an age of increased competition

Scouts develops skills for life; the character, practical and employability skills that young people will carry with them into adulthood, helping them to succeed.

Helping others

In times of crisis, Scouts across the world always rise to the challenge. From rescuing flood victims to supporting refugees, Scouts always try to follow the words of their promise to 'help other people'.

Cumbrian floods, UK

March 2016

When severe flooding affected large areas of Cumbria, England, Mike Davis, Assistant District Commissioner of Scouts for Duddon and High Furness, was one of the first to help. He was responsible for checking the water levels, which kept him busy through the night. Mike's team had the only vehicle that could access the main street, so they were able to check the welfare of those whose homes had been affected. They also delivered much-needed food supplies. Local Scouts then collected gifts from the community that they distributed to children who had been affected by the flooding.

Emergency First Aid, USA

May 2014

While hiking in Harriman State Park in New York, the Scouts from Troop and Crew 368 from Berkeley Heights, New Jersey, found a woman with an ankle injury. They thought her ankle was broken so constructed an improvised splint for her. They also made a stretcher using a tarpaulin and sticks, then transported her down the mountain where she was reunited with her husband and son. This reminds us that Scouts can help on both a large scale, and on a smaller scale, when individuals help out in their local communities in ways that change lives for the better.

Healthcare, Central African Republic

June 2018

Scouts were incredibly effective during the Ebola epidemic in the Central African Republic. Troops promoted vaccination, raised awareness about preventing disease and carried messages between rival military factions. 'We are here to make our country liveable and to stop the violence,' said Rony Yannick Bengai, the secretary general of the Catholic Scouts Association in the country. The Scouts and UNICEF signed a formal partnership in the country in 2017, and Scouts have been known to go from door to door, encouraging families to immunise.

Supporting refugees, Lesbos

September 2015

The Scouts of Greece crossed the Aegean Sea to the Greek island of Lesbos to offer their support and to help the refugee camps there. The Scouts spent time with the young people and their families in Mytilini, the main port, and at the refugee camp in Kara Tepe. Some played games and ran activities for children, while others helped clear the area of tonnes of waste.

Cave flood, Thailand

June 2018

The whole of the Scout movement was proud when John Volanthen, a Cub Scout Leader from the Long Ashton Scouts in Bristol, helped rescue 12 boys trapped in the Tham Luang caves in the Chiang Rai region of Thailand. Trained as a cave diver, John helped rescue 12 footballers aged between 11 and 16, and their coach. John was one of the first to reach the party, which at that point had been trapped for nine days. John and his team led the boys to safety through the waterlogged cave network. John received the Bronze Cross for 'heroism or action in the face of extraordinary risk', along with a letter from Chief Scout, Bear Grylls.

Supporting children, South Africa

November 2018

In Grassy Park, Cape Town, Scouts worked to provide disadvantaged young people with outdoor learning camps. They offered activities from using an axe safely, to building a suspension bridge, and useful First Aid.

Garret Dyantyi, the Springbok Patrol Leader in his Fezeka High School Troop in Cape Town, had to leave the Scouts for a while. He said: 'I was very sad when I had to quit because it was too dangerous for me to go to Scouts. There are a lot of gangs where I stay and it was not safe for me to walk to the Scout Hall. When they started Scouting at Fezeka High School last year I was so excited because it was now safe for me to come back and be a Scout.'

Future vision

There's a reason they called it the Scout movement – it changes with the times to stay relevant and meet the needs of young people.

A changing promise

The Scout movement has adapted over time, reacting and responding to the changing world around us. These changes can be seen in the Scout's Oath, which is now known as the Promise.

The original 1908 Scout Oath appeared in the first pamphlet of *Scouting for Boys*. It was:

'On my honour I promise that

1. I will do my duty to God and to the king
2. I will do my best to help others, whatever it costs me
3. I know the Scout law, and will obey it'.

Baden-Powell also introduced the Scout sign. He explained in the book that this would be made by holding up three fingers, which represented the three elements of the Promise.

The Promise has been revised many times to remain relevant and appropriate. In 1909, the words 'whatever it costs me' were changed to 'help other people at all times'. This was more in keeping with how Baden-Powell had originally phrased the oath in his manuscript for *Scouting for Boys*.

As the Scout movement spread around the world, elements of the Promise were adapted to suit the constitution of different countries. For example, Scouts in America make a promise to do their duty to their country, rather than to a monarch or a head of state.

As the UK became increasingly culturally diverse, different variations of the Promise were introduced to ensure that the movement was accessible to everyone.

In 1968, options for alternative wordings were created for people of other nationalities who lived in the UK: the phrase 'duty to the Queen' could be replaced with 'duty to the country in which I am now living'.

Variations were also created for Muslim, Hindu and Buddhist Scouts. In 2014, an alternative Promise was created for humanists and for those who do not follow a religion. In this version of the Promise, the 'duty to God' is substituted with a Promise to 'uphold Scout values'.

The Scout's Oath first appeared in Scouting for Boys in 1908.

The Scout Promise

On my honour, I promise that I will do my best,
To uphold our Scout values,
To do my duty to the Queen,
To help other people,
And to keep the Scout Law.

(For people with no affirmed faith or humanists aged 10½ to adult)

Several different versions of the Scout Promise are now available.

Scouts in the UK

By 2023 we will have prepared more young people with skills for life, supported by amazing leaders delivering an inspiring programme. The UK Scouts will be growing, more inclusive, shaped by young people and making a bigger impact in our communities. We want to:

Grow

We believe Scouts changes lives so we want to give every young person in the UK the opportunity to join.

Be more youth shaped

Every young person should be shaping their experience and developing their leadership potential.

Impact our communities

Through social action, Scouts makes a difference not just to the individual but to whole communities.

Become more inclusive

Everyone, regardless of their background, should be able to participate in Scouts.

The World Scout movement

The World Organization of the Scout Movement (WOSM) also has an inspiring vision for 2023:

'By 2023 Scouting will be the world's leading educational youth movement, enabling 100 million young people to be active citizens creating positive change in their communities and in the world based on shared values.'

There are six strategic priorities at world level to achieve this vision:

Youth engagement

Scouting should give young people the opportunity to develop skills and knowledge, empowering them to take an active part in the movement and in their communities. Involvement, recognition and intergenerational exchange are key in providing a framework for our youth members.

Communications and external relations

Scouting's profile should accurately portray what we do and why we do it, reflecting our shared values. By using the most impactful methods of communication, and engaging in strategically relevant partnerships, Scouting should be recognised as the world's leading youth movement.

Educational methods

The youth programme should provide a non-formal learning environment, strengthening the capacity of young people to face the challenges of tomorrow. Scouting should attract, train and retain quality adult volunteers to deliver the Youth Programme.

Social impact

Every Scout should be involved in community service, and share their experiences to inspire others. Through activities and projects, Scouts contribute to their communities and become leaders of positive change.

Diversity and inclusion

Scouting should reflect the societies in which it exists and actively work to welcome all individuals without distinction. This diversity should not only be reflected in the membership, but also the methods and programmes used within the movement.

Governance

The governance of WOSM should be transparent, accountable, efficient and clearly linked to its strategy, focused on achieving the vision of the movement. The roles and responsibilities in the organisation should be clearly defined and understood.

Into the future

Who knows what the Scouts of the future will do? Already there have been Scouts on the International Space Station, but will there one day be Scouts on Mars? While the badges and uniforms may change, the values and ethos of the Scouts are sure to remain the same: to work together, help other people, show our courage and kindness in everything we do.

While we wait for the next Scout to go into space, there's plenty more work to do down here on Earth. We're continuing to take Scouts to new and different people, especially those it could benefit the most. In the UK alone, we've opened over 1,280 new sections in deprived areas since 2014. We're working in places like Bow in east London, Tower Hamlets, inner-city Sheffield and Bristol with families who wouldn't have considered us before. We're basing ourselves in community centres and schools – going to where young people already are, rather than expecting them to come to us.

Scouts today might surprise you. We still help people in our community – we have 22,000 Scouts who are trained as Dementia Friends. But we also teach coding and have badges for snowboarding and geocaching. We don't just sit in tents all day waiting to light a fire – although we know how to do that too!

At the Scouts we know that childhood doesn't last forever. That's why we make it count. It's what you do early on that really matters. Learn how to take charge, play your part and speak up when you're young and those things will stay with you for life.

The outdoors is still the Scouts' natural home and the world's greatest classroom.

Appendices

Scouts around the world

Iceland
4,960

Denmark
43,282

Norway
21,815

Luxembourg
7,347

Belgium
107,243

Czechia
53,438

Ireland
49,385

Netherlands
55,011

UK
640,000

Ger...
117...

France
102,775

Switzerland
24,616

Austria
10,028

Monaco
87

Croatia
3,185

Portugal
81,366

Spain
72,973

Malta
3,100

Liechtenstein
635

Morocco
12,304

Tunisia
24,095

Mon...

Canada
98,204

Algeria
4,150

Senegal
9,857

Cabo
Verde
733

Mauritania
3,790

Ni...
3,3...

USA
3,399,147

Dominican
Republic
1,982

Honduras
3,250

Bahamas
1,540

Dominica
1,100

Saint Lucia
393

Guatemala
7,299

Haiti
43,618

Mexico
45,560

Aruba
487

Barbados
2,419

Nigeria
750,073

Jamaica
1,727

Saint Vincent
and the
Grenadines
230

El Salvador
3,608

Belize
874

Nicaragua
1,977

Venezuela
16,740

Curaçao
1,462

Gambia
15,582

Guinea
6,539

Liberia
2,418

Togo
10,747

Panama
2,494

Colombia
12,633

Grenada
1,378

Burkina
Faso
11,539

Ghana
3,919

Benin
7,229

Costa Rica
13,779

Guyana
424

Suriname
787

Trinidad
and Tobago
5,982

Sierra
Leone
16,162

Gab...
3,80...

Ecuador
10,031

Côte d'Ivoire
7,519

Peru
8,290

Brazil
90,102

Angola
18,830

Bolivia
7,355

Paraguay
1,086

Namibia
1,083

Uruguay
1,620

South
Africa
19,306

Chile
17,094

Argentina
69,637

Within just a few years of the camp on Brownsea Island, there were Scouts all over the world. Every few years, the WOSM conducts a census of how many Scouts there are in each country. These are the results of the last census, which took place in December 2016.

Finland	53,792
Sweden	36,398
Estonia	1,106
Latvia	872
Russian Federation	6,405
Lithuania	2,064
North Macedonia	2,191
Moldova	2,167
Belarus	1,050
Serbia	4,804
Armenia	2,255
Slovakia	7,831
Ukraine	12,335
Georgia	2,314
Azerbaijan	1,761
Kazakhstan	1,239
Mongolia	10,445
Bulgaria	890
San Marino	273
Turkey	141,277
Tajikistan	1,055
Bhutan	24,524
Scouts of China	56,182
Japan	109,687
Cyprus	5,890
Syria	9,358
Bahrain	1,800
Nepal	30,554
Hong Kong	98,190
Jordan	15,521
UAE	4,857
Pakistan	710,201
Republic of Korea	137,703
Egypt	83,610
Israel	83,332
India	3,647,843
Lebanon	15,410
Saudi Arabia	19,269
Kuwait	6,061
Palestine	33,643
Thailand	697,887
Brunei	2,570
Philippines	1,983,563
Papua New Guinea	4,980
Sudan	14,868
Yemen	6,481
Qatar	4,566
Oman	20,330
Sri Lanka	38,606
Myanmar	24,925
Cambodia	28,533
South Sudan	2,162
Ethiopia	68,001
Rwanda	18,884
Maldives	1,547
Fiji	10,175
Uganda	116,098
Kenya	1,312,485
Seychelles	286
Bangladesh	1,372,773
Indonesia	21,842,404
Burundi	28,559
Comoros	1,725
Singapore	11,439
Tanzania	538,959
Zambia	7,368
Malawi	50,020
Malaysia	70,714
Zimbabwe	18,312
Madagascar	50,599
Mauritius	5,509
Eswatini	6,850
Australia	67,668
Botswana	26,464
Mozambique	32,664
New Zealand	19,487
Kiribati	1,186
Lesotho	2,900

List of World Scout Jamborees

Year	Number	Location	Theme	Badge
1920	1st	Olympia, London, England	Develop world peace	There was no official badge in 1920.
1924	2nd	Ermelunden, Denmark	World citizenship	
1929	3rd	Arrowe Park, England	Coming of age	
1933	4th	Gödöllő, Hungary	Face new adventures	
1937	5th	Bloemendaal, Netherlands	Lead happy lives	
1947	6th	Moisson, France	Jamboree of peace	
1951	7th	Bad Ischl & Salzkammergut, Austria	Jamboree of simplicity	
1955	8th	Niagara-on-the-Lake, Canada	New horizons	
1957	9th	Sutton Park, England	50th anniversary of Scouting	
1959	10th	Laguna, Philippines	Building tomorrow today	
1963	11th	Marathon, Greece	Higher and wider	

1967	12th	Farragut State Park, USA	For friendship	
1971	13th	Shizuoka, Japan	For understanding	
1975	14th	Lillehammer, Norway	Five fingers, one hand	
1979		The World Scout Jamboree scheduled to take place in Iran was cancelled due to political unrest and was replaced by a series of World Scout Camps.		
1983	15th	Alberta, Canada	The spirit lives on	
1987/88	16th	Appin, Australia	Bringing the world together	
1991	17th	Kangwon, South Korea	Many lands, one world	
1995	18th	Dronten, Netherlands	Future is now	
1998/99	19th	Mostazal, Chile	Building peace together	
2002/03	20th	Chon Buri, Thailand	Share our world, share our cultures	
2007	21st	Chelmsford, England	One world, one promise	
2011	22nd	Rinkaby, Sweden	Simply Scouting	
2015	23rd	Kirara-hama, Yamaguchi City, Japan	A spirit of unity	
2019	24th	The Summit Bechtel Family National Scout Reserve, USA	Unlock a new world	

Index

Picture credits

Key:
t = top, b = bottom, l = left, r = right, m = middle. When images appear vertically, credits listed alphabetically, a–f.

The Scouts Heritage Service: 3tm, 3bl, 3br, 8–16, 17t, 17m, 18–24, 26–33, 34–58, 59br, 60–67, 68t, 68m, 68bl, 68br, 70, 71–107, 108b, 111t, 111bl, 111br, 112t, 114–115, 142, 143, 145tl, 145b, 184, 185, 186

The Scout Association: 3tl, 3tr, 3bm, 6, 116tl, 116tr, 116ml, 116mr, 116bl, 118–128, 131t, 133t, 135t, 138–140, 144, 145tr, 147, 156, 158t, 158m, 159t, 160, 162–170, 171tl, 174–179

Shutterstock: 25, 59tl, 59tr, 59bl, 130, 131b, 132b, 133b, 134b, 135, 148, 151b, 151c, 151d, 155, 157, 158b, 159b

© World Scout Bureau Inc.: 108t, 109, 110, 112b, 137, 146, 171tr

Getty images: 132t, 150, 151e, 152, 153

Alamy: 116br, 134t

18th Bromley Scouts: 151a

16th Allerton (St Aiden) Scouts: 154

John Palmer (public domain): 17b

© 2010 Lestaret: 34t

Cecil Stoughton, White House (public domain): 159m

Isle of Wight Scout Council: 69

Martyn Milner: 147

MSFC, NASA: 136

Front cover, clockwise from top left: The Scout Association, The Scouts Heritage Service, The Scout Association, The Scouts Heritage Service, The Scout Association, The Scouts Heritage Service.

Back cover: clockwise from top left: The Scout Association, The Scouts Heritage Service, The Scout Association, The Scouts Heritage Service, The Scout Association, The Scouts Heritage Service,

Acknowledgements

The publisher would like to thank everyone who contributed to this book: Chris James, Caroline Pantling, Caroline Hamson, Peter Ford, Cara Davies and Thomas Robertson at the Scouts; Bear Grylls, the Scout Ambassadors, the Scout Adventurers; Martyn Milner, Dave Bird and Paul Kubalek for photography; Victor Ortega at the World Scout Bureau; Sophie Blackman, Rob Ward, Laura Pollard, Jessica Read and Ruth Ellis.

What we do

We're Scouts and everyone's welcome here. All genders, races and backgrounds. Every week we give almost half a million people aged 6-25 the skills they need for school, college, university, the job interview, the important speech, the tricky challenge and the big dreams: the skills they need for life.

'Scouts made me a do-er and a give it a go-er. Made me question and listen and have a wide-open mind. Scouts made me take a deep breath and speak up. Made me think on my feet, made me see the big picture, made me ignore the butterflies and go for it. Scouts made me get back up and try again. Made me think about what's next, and plan for it. Made me jump in, get muddy, give back and get set.'

Thinking about volunteering

Scouts is only possible thanks to our incredible volunteers. They have as much fun and learn as many skills as our young people. Find out how you can get involved and give as much or as little time as you want.

Further reading

scouts.org.uk
shop.scouts.org.uk
scoutadventures.org.uk
scout.org